ADVANCE PRAISE

"Very informative and on the money, dealing with the behaviours and actions required to get a data culture working that will deliver real business benefits. I'm already modifying & tweaking my own behaviours and interactions, excellent stuff!"

Lee Taylor, Senior Insights Expert, Shell

"I believe *Seeing Around Corners* is the most relevant business book I have read this year. Every leader should read this; whether they are in a start-up or major corporation. It is a book for now, and one that gives you confidence in a period of such uncertainty and disruption."

Mark Sutherland, Chief Technology Officer, Capita plc

"The evolution of 'Big Data' and advanced analytics is not about data or information technology, it's about rethinking the fundamentals about how we lead and manage organizations. It has the potential to be the biggest force to shape organizations since the industrial revolution. *Seeing Around Corners* brings to life the transformational potential of the new data paradigm and powerfully demonstrates the need to re-think how leaders make decisions. A must read for anyone who wants to be a leader in any organization."

Dr. Mark Powell, UK Head of Insights and Data, Capgemini Ltd

"*Seeing Around Corners* is the how-to guide for a modern data driven business leader, with brilliant first-hand experiences from Hogg, linked to real pearls of wisdom with fascinating real-world business examples. The chapter on Messy Teams is genius. This is the must-read business book of the year."

Paul Brook, Director Data Analytics EMEA, Dell EMC

"In his timely release of *Seeing Around Corners*, Graham Hogg nails it! Graham artfully exposes the 'sufficient conditions' required to accelerate value of invested technologies. His style is both engaging and thought provoking, using a rich collection of examples drawn from personal experience as a Royale Marines Intelligence Officer and extensive interviews with recognized business leaders. Graham is a story teller, covering the often politically contentious, mission critical enabler, resulting from alignment of individuals-teams-organizations to the achievement of their higher 'purpose' in a well-balanced perspective in the words of key stakeholders who've lived it."

Bill Lombardi, Global Sales & Delivery Executive, Watson AI

"Graham has written an important book about how CEOs and corporate leaders can make the most of data in an era where we are drowning in information and gasping to use it wisely. It addresses a critical contemporary concern for leaders to master the rich potential of data, and goes beyond the technical to address the bigger business concepts of purpose, strategy and teamwork. Graham creates a new and vivid language of data that is important for any of today's leaders to master."

Tom Andrews, President of Organizational Transformation, SYPartners

"At a time when companies have never been more vulnerable to disruption, the ability to peek into the future and prepare in advance for rapid change is critical. It's in that context that *Seeing Around Corners* offers such a refreshing perspective on big data. Hogg makes an important contribution to an already hot topic, and one I'm sure I'll find myself returning to many times in the months and years to come for a source of inspiration."

Nigel Miller, Chief HR Officer, Edelman

"*Seeing Around Corners* offers a fresh perspective on what it takes for analytics to fulfil its promise. It's the best book on analytics I've ever read, because it really sets out how to put analytics at the centre of strategy."

James Walker, Partner, Global Head of Analytics,
OC&C Strategy Consultants

"Success in today's data-driven world cannot be achieved with yesterday's thinking. Based on Graham's extensive experience in the Royal Marines and business, *Seeing Around Corners* shows how leaders and their teams can use data to see emerging threats and opportunities sooner and reap the benefits faster."

Dr Arnoud Franken, Senior Consultant, InContext Consultancy Group, Visiting Fellow, Cranfield University.

"Graham is a great exponent of the culture organizations need to embrace to get the best from data. Too often data and analytics is seen as a task for 'the few' but this book shows us that it is a fundamental skill for leaders to embrace with everyone, every day. If you are looking to learn and drive change in a complex and fast moving world you will find insight and great examples here."

Simon Hay, Former CEO, Dunhumby

"Like many data people, I come from a technical background and approach to data, yet the most consistent message coming out as we drown in data today is how do you sift through the masses and create business value. *Seeing Around Corners* demonstrates how to do that quickly and consistently day in day out across your business."

Graeme McDermott, Chief Data Officer, Addison Lee

"A fantastic read, really getting under the skin of why organizations operate in silos and why asking better questions of our data can help us work across them and drive value."

Mike Rose, Head of Data Engagement, Department for Environment, Food and Rural Affairs, UK Government

"Combining experiences from the author's time in Afghanistan with powerful corporate examples, *Seeing Around Corners* is a practical guide to changing the way your company thinks about and acts on data. Recommended for anyone looking to build a data-driven culture across their business."

Ryan Den Rooijen, Head of Data, Dyson

Published by
LID Publishing Limited
The Record Hall, Studio 204,
16-16a Baldwins Gardens,
London EC1N 7RJ, UK

524 Broadway, 11th Floor, Suite 08-120
New York, NY 10012, US

info@lidpublishing.com
www.lidpublishing.com

A member of:

www.businesspublishersroundtable.com

Printed in Great Britain by TJ International
ISBN: 978-1-911498-48-3

Cover and page design: Caroline Li

SEEING
AROUND
CORNERS

HOW TO UNLOCK THE POTENTIAL OF BIG DATA

GRAHAM HOGG

LID

LONDON   MONTERREY
MADRID   SHANGHAI
MEXICO CITY   BOGOTA
NEW YORK   BUENOS AIRES
BARCELONA   SAN FRANCISCO

CONTENTS

*"This book is dedicated to the people
who mean the most to me:
Chevaun and Reeva."*

March 8th, 2019

Andrew,

I hope you enjoy the pages that follow — I look forward to meeting you in-person.

"Hoofing"

Graham Hogg

War is an incredible teacher …
and it teaches you lessons
that you will not forget.

Jocko Willink
Former US Navy Seal
and recipient of the Silver Star and Bronze Star
for his service in the Iraq War

ACKNOWLEDGEMENTS

It has always been and will continue to be a privilege and honour to have served my country, and it is to the brave men and women with whom I served that I would like to share my gratitude for writing this book. Together, we have learned many lessons that I believe have made us all stronger as a result. Your work and commitment continue to inspire me to help others be better.

I am also grateful to the hundreds of business executives and teams that I have had the pleasure to meet and talk with around a subject that we all have an unlimited passion for. Thank you for your dedicated time, insights and commitment to unlocking the potential of your data and your teams within the great companies that you work in.

I am also grateful for the academic support that I have received throughout the process, from business school leaders and experts in their respective fields.

Thank you to my business partner and friend Toby Hunt. Your leadership took the strain of the business when it was most needed, allowing me to escape to the confines of my writing. Your daily challenges inspire me and our diversity of thought is our competitive advantage; one coffee at a time!

To my parents who gave me all the love that a young man could have ever needed to go out and discover the world, knowing you would provide me with safety when I needed it.

And finally, to my amazing Chevaun. For the encouragement and motivation during those early mornings and late nights, from the very first page to the last. Everything I do is for you.

INTRODUCTION

The Bamiyan highway dissecting through the city of Kandahar in Afghanistan is mostly straight. Small bazaars on either side of the road buzz with activity, with locals going about their business, mostly ignoring the presence of the British military convoys charging through on their daily routines. I recall the city having a distinct smell: wet dirt mixed with diesel from old truck engines that had seen better days, bellowing smoke as they attempted to push and grind through the traffic.

Years later, while walking along a sidewalk on a wet morning on the Lower East Side of New York City, I would pass by a construction site and the smell of fuel and dirt would bring back memories of those journeys through Kandahar.

The roads in Kandahar were greasy and wet, not presenting any significant challenge to our vehicles. But every so often, due to the poor sewage system in the city, we were confronted by a flooded area of the road that would cause one of our drivers to slow down and guide their heavy vehicle through – trying to prevent the engine from being flooded or, even worse, causing the long line of vehicles behind it to slow down.

On each side of the road, in distinctive sections, were three-foot concrete dividers, forcing vehicles to navigate to one side or the other. This had a channelling effect and reduced our ability to swerve to the other side of the road if the situation required it.

During the unrelenting heat of the Afghan summer, when temperatures often soared to 40°C in the city, clouds of dust would rise up as traffic trundled along the broken roads, limiting drivers' ability to see. It was OK for the locals, who knew every crack in the pavement, but it presented more of a challenge for foreigners.

Kandahar was dominated by a low din of activity: honking car horns, tired engines crawling through traffic like old men, workers banging away at pieces of metal, people wrestling through their daily challenges. On that day, though, the roar of British Land Rovers added to the cacophony of noise, as they accelerated up and down the roads of the city. As the leader that day, I was fixed to the sound coming from my radio headset, doing my best to keep a gentle hand on the flow of the convoy and let my team do their job of getting us through safely. I recall having light conversations with my driver about everything from what was going on at the time, to friends and family back home, and getting to the end of the tour. It was a brief respite from the mayhem surrounding us.

Often, the architecture of the surrounding buildings took me by surprise. Beautiful structures, distracting me momentarily, with colourful shutter windows or exotic frontages, contrasted against the harsh, rugged hills just behind. Kites occasionally filled the sky; the array of blue, white, red and gold colours was a nice contrast against the grey Kandahar sky. I was all too aware that these weren't necessarily being flown by innocent children, but were often used to signal our approach by people with a more menacing goal. Occasionally we'd get the attention of children who would offer a smile or wave as we exchanged looks. But generally, having been brought up in a war-torn country, these generations of Afghans weren't too interested in us.

The vast number of vehicles on the streets featured many different shapes and sizes, with some brands and models familiar to us, others less so. Toyota pickup trucks filled with goats and farm workers trundled by, while local policeman and members of the Afghanistan National Army exchanged knowing looks as they raced past.

Donkeys pulled carts that looked like they were going to topple over at any moment under the weight and strain of their load, and three-wheeled rickshaws transported Burqa-clad women. Typical to that part of the world were even smaller modes of transportation: young boys navigating heavily loaded wheelbarrows and motorcyclists weaved between traffic like bees collecting honey.

That Sunday morning as we entered Kandahar, the second-largest city in Afghanistan, with a population of around half a million[1] going about its morning business, we did so from the east. The route selection had to allow for our entire convoy of 40 vehicles, and more than 60 marines and soldiers, to pass through without getting split up, while allowing us to maintain speed and momentum. It wasn't easy to avoid narrow streets and built-up areas. We knew that if we found ourselves in slow-moving traffic and were forced to reduce our pace, we'd become extremely vulnerable to attack. To help us navigate, we were assisted by a Lynx helicopter flying above us. I could talk to its crew whenever I needed to, seeking advice on potential roadblocks ahead or to provide the required support of casualty evacuations if the situation arose.

Our task was to provide force protection for a logistical convoy moving from Kandahar to Helmand Province, containing critical supplies for British troops fighting in Helmand to the west. Our footprint on the ground was significant – some of the vehicles weighed more than 40 tonnes and crawled at a maximum speed of 20km an hour when fully loaded with equipment. As we stretched out across the road that morning, we made up a serpent-like figure stretching over two kilometres from head to tail.

1 Wikipedia, "Kandahar," last modified July 31, 2017 https://en.wikipedia.org/wiki/Kandahar

NAVIGATING COMPLEXITY

The intelligence picture we received at that time pointed to a threat coming from Vehicle-Born Improvised Explosive Devices (VBIEDs). This was predicted to manifest as a suicide bomber on a motorcycle, car or bicycle, with explosives attached to some sort of self-detonating device. This picture, although somewhat broad, allowed us to adapt our tactics to a degree. *Keep moving, look ahead and keep traffic away from the convoy.* This was a challenging task with the complexity and chaos of the city in front of us that day. Navigating around the city to the north or south would have been a preferable option, but due to the limited off-road capability of the larger vehicles, our route was selected for us.

We knew that our vulnerability was our size. We were a big and slow-moving target, faced with a small and nimble enemy who had little to lose. As a young man responsible for the lives of the men and women in the convoy, I had a horrible feeling about this trip.

We had been delayed leaving the base that morning for a reason that now escapes me, but as we focused on the 150km journey ahead of us, I found myself thinking about home; with Christmas drawing near, I was feeling a bit homesick. As the minutes ticked away that morning, the city was slowly starting to fill with local vehicles going about their daily business, making what was in front of us an increasingly complex challenge to navigate.

Soon enough, my signaller ran around the side of our command vehicle, saying, "We're good to go, boss," and within minutes, the sound of 40 roaring diesel engines filled the air. We turned out of the airfield base, under a gloomy Afghan sky, and slowly crept towards the bristling activity of Kandahar.

The situation in Afghanistan during that time could be described as highly complex. The notion of "good guys, bad guys and civilians" that had held water in previous, less complex, military conflicts no longer provided decision makers with the required detailed intelligence picture. Indigenous security forces, local militias and criminal networks all had to be routinely monitored in pursuit of identifying insurgent targets and threats. This wasn't simply a case of conducting a deep dive into the situation and then presenting a report, but building a continuously evolving picture to allow decision makers to adapt and innovate around their plans.

We were faced with a situation where a shifting population could be influenced by multiple factors at varying times to varying degrees. When faced with such complexity and uncertainty, the organization that could connect intelligence and data to decision makers in the most relevant and timely way possessed the greatest chance of success. It wasn't a case of how much data was available – as this was increasingly growing in volume – the challenge was that of validity, finding out what was relevant. It was about what data needed to get where, to whom and by when.

Adding to this complexity, the number of NATO forces providing security to Afghanistan at the time and throughout the period was vast as shown in Figure 1.

FIGURE 1: SOURCED FROM OPERATION ENDURING FREEDOM COUNTRY MAP

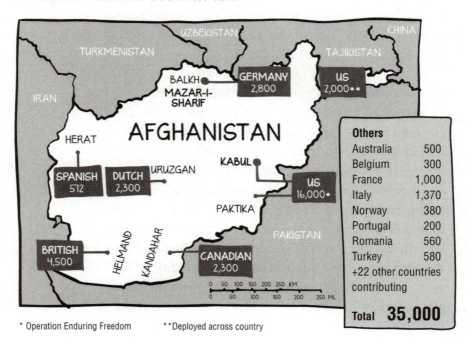

* Operation Enduring Freedom   **Deployed across country

In just the two provinces of Helmand and Kandahar that we were navigating, 7-10 NATO Security Nations also were conducting operations in the same areas – under the same command structure. This presented a significant challenge when it came to data and intelligence flows. Due to the hierarchical nature of leadership in the military, the deeper you went into the organization, the more the intelligence picture became siloed. At the highest executive level, they had multiple intelligence and data-collection assets available to them. Firstly was human intelligence, in which field human-intelligence teams liaised with local businessmen, non-governmental organizations (NGOs) and tribesmen to obtain insights into situations as they evolved. Secondly, signals intelligence could be used to analyse a conversation between two or more people, during which the motivations and considerations of their relationships could be taken into consideration. In Afghanistan at that time, open-source intelligence, such as local media, was highly valuable to gauge local opinion. Imagery, geospatial and technical intelligence all contributed, as well.

My role, probably six layers below the broadest regional intelligence picture that I allude to above, was to lead the convoy from point A to B, as shown in Figure 2.

FIGURE 2: OPERATION RITA ROUTE MAP

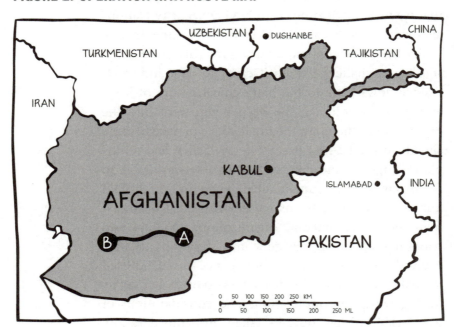

This was a 150km route from the Kandahar airfield base, through the city and Panjwai District – a Canadian area of operations – and then west to the British area of operations in Helmand Province. Adding further complexity to this route was our need to pass through Gereshk, a small town to the east of Helmand Province where another British team was running operations. The intelligence environment meant that we were faced with multiple commanders and areas of operational responsibility, networked with defined areas of data and intelligence interest. The route we took that morning crossed all intersections, presenting a fragmented picture.

My focus leading up to that day was that of an efficient execution of the mission. Following what I had been taught, our performance around casualty evacuation, vehicle handling, navigation, weapons handling, communication procedure – I could go on – was excellent. The skill and experience of our team was world-class and I had every confidence that they could overcome the challenges we faced.

SEEING AROUND CORNERS

The explosion felt like a hard thud against my chest. I remember the huge cloud of smoke and what seemed like small bits of debris flying everywhere in slow motion, as if I were watching it on a screen. Time slowed down, and as I checked myself and then my driver next to me, I realized what had just happened.

We had just been hit by an Improvised Explosive Device – an IED.

A vehicle laden with explosives, fragmented metal objects and debris had driven into a vehicle in the convoy and detonated the device, blowing up the Land Rover third from the front. Thankfully, the bomb was poorly constructed and the majority of the blast went into the ground; if it had been differently engineered, it would have presented a very different story. Three men were injured.

What followed was a superbly executed casualty evacuation procedure from members of my team, with very little direction from me. This high-performing team's efficiency and professionalism kicked in like nothing I had ever seen. As we had rehearsed and planned numerous times previously, the final vehicle in the convoy collected the casualties and evacuated them to a safe area in the city, a school playing field where the helicopter could land, all under the command of a junior leader of the team. Members of that evacuation team showed composure and courage navigating across the city alone, while at the same time they were monitoring and providing medical support to three of their injured comrades. That same team then found me, and the rest of the convoy, on the other side of the city, where we linked up and continued with the mission. What needs to be remembered from this story is the superb professionalism and courage of those who faced that extremely challenging situation.

FROM "WHAT DO I NEED TO DO?" TO "WHAT DO I NEED TO KNOW?"

I woke up the next morning in the familiar surroundings of the British camp in Southern Helmand feeling distinctly low, but what followed has since shaped my thinking. After breakfast, I walked across the camp to visit one of the injured team members at the camp hospital. His injuries were minimal and we exchanged accounts of what had happened the day before. After a cup of tea, I walked across to the other side of the camp to talk to a friend and colleague in the data centre. Immediately, I could tell he had something to say. It was clear that we had left the Kandahar airfield that morning at the wrong time. All the data pointed towards suicide-bombing activity spiking between 10am and midday in that area. We got hit at 10.03am.

The data that was being modelled at the highest level was from human intelligence, from operatives on the ground sharing what they were seeing in the area, to more complicated unstructured data sets such as DNA samples, social media tip-offs and other biometric

INTRODUCTION

INTRODUCTION // PART ONE /// CHAPTER 1 /// CHAPTER 2 /// CHAPTER 3 /// CHAPTER 4 /// PART TWO /// CHAPTER 5 /// CHAPTER 6 /// CHAPTER 7 /// PART THREE /// CHAPTER 8 /// CHAPTER 9 /// CHAPTER 10 /// CONCLUSION

data from previous attacks. Using state-of-the-art technology, they could see clearly where the threats and opportunities were across the battlefield.

None of this information had found its way in to my planning and decision-making.

When I asked about what else we could have done, he turned to me and pointed to the American and Canadian tactics. "They run all of their convoys at night," he said. I challenged him that we had visited this option month earlier, but driving a 40-tonne vehicle at night using night vision equipment was impossible.

He explained that there was a curfew in Kandahar and that no locals were allowed out in the city after 10pm. You could drive through with your lights on and engines roaring at full speed and no one would get in your way – the local police and army would even coordinate and support such movement.

This allowed me to connect experience and data from another team in the organization to my decision-making. The following convoys were run at night with no incident after our return to the UK.

IT ALL COMES DOWN TO THIS

It's hard to escape the excitement around big data, but if it fails to be anchored into everyday important decisions across an organization, all opportunity will go to waste.

This book is how organizations, teams and individuals can close the gap between the production and consumption of data:

- To align data collection to what's important in every team, supported by leadership.
- To move away from command-and-control leadership styles and ivory-tower analytics, towards empowering teams to ask better questions to data.
- To challenge assumptions, groupthink and bias.

We'll explore how leaders can take action based on analytics results, *building* on their own domain expertise to innovate and adapt. I discuss how it's through the middle management of organizations – who are closer to customers, clients, patients or consumers – that the exponential benefit of advanced analytics can be realized. By applying analytics to the most important decisions, at the most important times, through a shared language or 'leaps of faith' because the situation demands it, you will make the best use of analytic skills in your organizations and make the best decisions.

To move away from an execution mindset and on to having a discovery mindset, it is essential to build a more connected organizational decision-making and data capability. This is not a technical challenge for organizations and leaders alone, but rather a cultural one, to break data silos and share insights across team boundaries.

When organizations get this right, data will be the source of adaptability, so that they can be a step ahead of change, risk and growth before the competition – so they can see around corners.

WHY IS SEEING AROUND CORNERS IMPORTANT?

Never, in modern history, have companies been so vulnerable to disruption. Failure to adapt to rapid change, failure to address disruption, and adopting to a more complex international economic environment – all these pressures and more are causing what were once large, dominant blue-chip companies to turn into penny shares.

Recent research[2] shows that, in 1965, the average tenure of companies on the American stock market index, Standard & Poor's 500 (S&P 500), was 33 years. By 1990, it was 20 years. It's forecast to shrink to 14 years by 2026, according to Harvard Business School Professor Clayton Christensen. And, about 50% of the S&P 500 are expected to be replaced over the next 10 years.

2 Paul Hobcraft, "Hobcraft Innovation Report," (no month or day) 2016, last accessed on August 25, 2017 https://cdn2. hubspot.net/ hubfs/314186/ Content/Papers_ Reports_Booklets/ Hobcraft_Seeking_ Change_from_ Innovation_2016/ Hobcraft_Seeking_ Change_from_ Innovation_ in_2016_ webversion.pdf

27

Technological innovation is only a small part of the disruption that is putting a stake through the heart of these companies. Certainly, the emergence of smartphones and other mobile devices, live data feeds coming from the Internet of Things (the growing network of physical objects with an IP address for internet connectivity and communication between those devices and systems) and companies' increasing ability to make use of big data with analytics are all raising the bar for existing companies.

But, often, it is actually management's inability to keep up with trends, and a too-rigid organizational structure that prevents reaction to detected trends, which leads to failure.

For example, many companies invest in setting up the equipment required for analysing big data, but then they fail to establish a meaningful framework for obtaining usable insights from it. Or there are the companies that become very good at analysis, but that can't implement the conclusions of the insights in day-to-day operations.

The result is that analysts have forecast about $50 trillion in stock-market value going up in smoke in the coming five years. Having an established market position is no longer sufficient to survive. The companies that fail will be replaced by disruptors like Uber and Airbnb that know how to draw key insights from data.

During research for this book, I spoke to Riley Newman, the Chief Data Officer at Airbnb – a company that has grown to a valuation of more than $30 billion and has arguably disrupted an industry overnight. Data and insights are at the centre of this amazing story. He told me how, proportionately, they're the largest data company in the world – in terms of the ratio between data scientists to employees.

In the company's early stages, the founders were able to go and have 'living-room conversations' with their customers, to understand their needs and pains. During these early start-up days, they were able to combine what they were hearing and seeing on the front line with the company's own purpose.

A data-driven culture now enables them to scale this purpose, where they can keep the organization in a tight relationship with their customer base, hearing what people want and responding to it – at scale!

"Airbnb is a start-up that has the clear purpose of letting people 'belong anywhere' – you can see the tale of two start-ups that have gone from nothing to something significant," comments management expert Alicia Hare of SYPartners. "Airbnb has been very thoughtful from the beginning, though, as the organization has a clear purpose and culture, and has been effective in navigating the big challenges they've faced by relying on those central tenets."

All companies have a moment when they have to reconnect to their true purpose, Hare points out. Whether it's a crisis situation or a leadership change, all organizations experience disruptive moments. What's helpful during these moments is to have an anchor and to use it to imagine what future they want to create next. This offers the opportunity to move beyond the fear of running out of ideas and puts the company in a position of creativity, activation and positive impact.

In this world of heightened complexity, organizations' ability to gain an accurate picture of their future conditions is of critical importance. Predicting customer needs, client pains or human capital demands, just to name a few key areas, has become a win-or-lose capability for businesses today. All companies can collect data – in the information age, technology and the access to data is available to all at an increasingly low cost. But only the organizations that can gain a heightened level of *understanding* from data will be successful.

This is not about the best dashboard or data visualization in class, but connecting data to leadership experience on the front line.

Organizations like Kodak and Nokia have shown that an organization's ability to understand what is happening in the market is of critical importance. In this new age, understanding trumps execution every time.

Collecting big data, drawing useful insights from it, and connecting that knowledge to expertise is the great opportunity companies have to succeed today, but it is also their biggest challenge. Fostering a data-driven culture and implementing data-driven decisions every day throughout the business is the way forward – to see around corners.

PART ONE
BUILDING A DATA-DRIVEN CULTURE

The biggest aspect of implementing a data-driven culture is culture. It's not a matter of a platitudinous corporate culture: Companies must focus on their purpose, a set of words that defines why they exist in the world, pointing to those they serve. Their strategic goals get them there, but teams must ask *what they need to know* in order to build value against their purpose. This cultural homiletic must be combined with an external focus on customers, the market and what is happening to both in real time. Data from consumer behaviours and market trends must get to the teams closest to the front line, who must build the right thinking skills, enabling them to conduct analysis using datasets available to them and translate this back to the centre. The front line must learn a new way of thinking, where coming up with the right questions is more important than flawless execution, challenging assumptions, groupthink and bias in every meeting.

Here, leaders must learn to understand when they need to 'get on the roof', that is, remove themselves from day-to-day activity and engage with analytics to see what is coming next. Leaders need to connect their experience with this data to build a heightened level of foresight, and they need to learn how to derive business value from it. This will become increasingly important in the world of information overload.

When these changes come together, *data-driven discovery* will grow throughout the teams in your organization. It is this pervasive curiosity – at all levels – that enables teams to adapt and uncover new areas of growth and opportunity and measure them against what matters most.

CHAPTER 1
PURPOSE AND DISCOVERY

Profit isn't a purpose, it's a result.
To have purpose means the things
we do are of real value to others.

Simon Sinek
Author, *Start With Why*

The starting point for an organization, irrespective of size, is purpose; this guides behaviour and decisions every day and informs successful companies. As organizations seek to build a data-driven culture, purpose is the anchor point at which they must start.

Here's how starting with a well-defined purpose makes it all happen.

I remember looking at the pile of young bodies with smiling faces in front of me, covered in mud from head to toe, eagerly waiting for their next instruction at the sound of my whistle. I had no idea where the ball was, or how we had come to this situation, but I knew that the 12 or so young boys and girls playing rugby that day were having the time of their lives – mud and all!

To be honest, my biggest concern when coaching rugby in the midst of the Indian monsoon in Kolkata was drowning. Following the rains, huge puddles formed in spots around the field, so that as soon as play gravitated that way, everything slowed down, and the importance of the possession of the ball, the scoreboard or the opposition were all lost to the fun and excitement of the mud and water – slipping and sliding your way between friend and foe. It was just the unfortunate player trapped at the bottom of the pile of bodies who at times needed to be rescued. As I reached into the fray and pulled the small body coughing and spluttering dirty water from his or her mouth, I was always greeted with a beaming smile. A quick pat on the back and then I tossed them back into the mayhem.

My fondest memory was seeing the enthusiasm and excitement in the children as soon as they caught the ball – which, more often than not, was larger than their tiny bodies. But with strong bare feet holding them up, and the open ground in front of them, nothing else mattered apart from running as fast as they could towards the line. I often had to point out where the lines were through the long, unkempt grass of the Maiden Park in Kolkata, with the Victoria Memorial offering a majestic backdrop and the sound of taxi horns cheering the children along as they sprinted past.

This was a place where gender, age or any other of life's quandaries didn't matter, where former Kolkata street children could run and pass and tackle and wrestle with friends without a care in the world. Here they were free, and they could be anything that they wanted to be.

It is with immense pride that I was part of this story. The purpose: providing children with the fundamentals of a normal life.

The organization that I was working for during that Indian monsoon season had, for the previous 20 years, provided homes and accommodation for the children of the city of Kolkata, India. These were children who had seen a hard start in life as orphans or been driven from their homes by abuse, family breakdown or extreme poverty.

Homes were set up by the charity, along with schooling and education, always driven by the purpose of providing children with the fundamentals of a normal life.

The organization achieved this through a series of clearly defined values and behaviours. These were carefully articulated and published for all to see, so that they informed the thoughts and actions of the members of the organization every day. These were:

- Provide a sense of belonging and security for the children.
- Ensure that the children can be with people they can trust and depend on.
- Ensure that the children are healthy and well-fed.
- Have the children laugh and play.
- Explore the children's talents and creativity.
- Provide education.

As you read through these, you will notice the common theme in each of them is the children. None of these refer to the organization; instead, they all refer to the 'significant others', the children.

I personally felt connected to this purpose. Not to all of it, as I was aware of the complexity of what the organization was trying to achieve, but to just one small part – 'to laugh and play'.

I knew that I wasn't able to teach them math, or cater to their health needs, but I knew that I could really add to this small part of their lives. And I knew how important it was in relation to the other parts. All I had to do was ensure that when I took the children out onto the playing field, they ran, smiled and had fun – and obviously didn't drown! And when the alarm clock went off at 5am, it was this thought that motivated the other coaches and me, what guided and inspired us through every action.

PURPOSE IS WHERE WE START WITH DATA

Purpose is where everything begins in an organization. This is not a plan, or a strategic goal, but the overreaching higher ideal that guides efforts and choices made by the teams within it. It defines why the organization exists in the world and stays true to its mission. It does not change over time, irrespective of turbulence or hardship. It informs every team's ambitions, wherever they are or with whatever they are trying to achieve – human resources, operations, sales or strategy, and across geographic boundaries.

When building a data-driven culture, start with your significant others, not data. The organization I use as the example above has a noble social purpose that naturally spurs support. Charities all over the world achieve this, which is why people volunteer to work for them and donate money to their cause.

Achieving this kind of attachment to purpose at a commercial organization is more difficult. But successful organizations achieve an externally oriented purpose that informs the actions of their teams every day. This purpose is critical in the creation of a data-driven organization. Later, we'll see how purpose becomes a handrail for data-driven discovery.

Relying on yesterday's advantage will kill you tomorrow. An external orientation is more important today for organizations than it has ever been.

We didn't do anything wrong,
but somehow, we lost.

Stephen Elop
CEO, Nokia

However an organization chooses to define its purpose, there should be a fundamental attempt to make a difference in the lives of other people or organizations.

Every team in every department in every meeting must be focused on others – on the difference that can be made in their lives.

In his TED talk, Adam Leipzig, CEO of Entertainment Media Partners[3], suggests a way of delineating this purpose. He asks the question, "How do you find your life's purpose in five minutes?"

Leipzig tells a story about going to a 20th-year class reunion with his Yale college friends. He was surprised to find that the majority of them were unhappy. Sure, they had great jobs and great houses and fine lifestyles, but 80% of the group was unhappy nonetheless, as they had no real purpose in life.

Having thought about this, he came up with these five questions that can help to identify the purpose in one's life:

1. Who are you?
2. What do you do?
3. Who are you doing it for?
4. What is it that those people need or want?
5. How are their lives going to be changed or transformed as a result of what you do for them?

3 Adam Leipzig, "Ted Talk," May 5, 2016, last accessed August 25, 2017 https://tedxinnovations. ted.com/2016/05/16/ adam-leipzig-only-needs-five-minutes-to-help-you-find-your-life-purpose/

Leipzig notes that the majority of questions, the final three, are about other people, *outward facing*. Only two of the five are about self-reflecting. He goes on to describe how the happiest and most successful people are those who serve others and know exactly whom they serve, what these people need, and how these people can be changed for the better as a result of their work, products or services.

Leipzig found that those who have focused their life's work on service to others – for example, teachers and professionals in academia or the arts – are the happiest. And those who are the most successful in their respective fields are those who have focused on others, not themselves.

Organizations are the same, and those that take this perspective have a long record of success. For example, the financial services company ING states its purpose as, "Empowering people to stay a step ahead in life and in business."

The Kellogg Company's mission is to, "Nourish families so they can flourish and thrive."

Notice here the recurring theme of external orientation; that is, thinking about others – people, families. This isn't just sentiment. This is hard-headed, commercial thinking. Harley Davidson's purpose is, "Fulfilling dreams of personal freedom." Facebook seeks "to make the world more connected."

Consider the example of Intercontinental Hotels: "Great hotels that *guests* love."

In establishing its purpose, Intercontinental Hotels talk about 'guests', not customers. The reasoning was simple. When someone you don't know knocks at the door, you are cautious, careful and not necessarily welcoming. But if a guest knocks at the door, you open it wide, invite them in, talk and offer drinks.

By treating their customers as guests, Intercontinental Hotels changed the way the entire organization behaved. 'Customers' are people you do business with, and so you think in terms of how to make money from them. But guests are people you care about.

Employees started thinking about how to make guests comfortable, how to receive them thoughtfully, and what amenities would make guests happy; their thoughts and actions were all targeted towards their guests. It's a simple but powerful example of how important language can be in formulating an outward-facing orientation – through your purpose.

The hotel group went further and even talked about 'love' for their guests. A word not often used in business, but used in the sense of 'my family', whom you know intimately and show love for.

What do they like to read? What sort of music do they enjoy as they walk through the hotel lobby? What type of food do they enjoy? How important is hot, fresh coffee to them as they start their day?

Most of all, employees understood that they didn't want to let guests down. It wasn't a question of performing certain tasks guests wanted, but of making sure that everything at the hotel contributed to their comfort and well-being – an unconditional discovery to stay ahead of guest needs.

So, it becomes clear how organizations are informed by their purpose to drive curiosity about how to improve performance. At the end of the day, this is all that counts.

Herb Kelleher founded Southwest Airlines with the purpose of providing an affordable option to the vast proportion of the US population who could not afford to fly. He built a corporate culture based around the customers' needs, so that the purpose informed the entire workforce and drove discovery. As Southwest Airlines announces consecutive years of profitability, competitors scramble to catch up.

In a similar example, Howard Schultz returned to Starbucks as CEO in 2008 to focus the company around its original purpose: "Great coffee for customers and a warm space for networking." What followed was the closure of more than 7,000 stores to re-engage employees to the Starbucks' experience. At the end of 2009, with a clear and simple purpose, Starbucks had tripled its earnings.[4]

4 Catalyst Investments, "Starbucks, more than just a coffee shop," Seeking Alpha, April 10, 2013 last accessed on August 25, 2017 https://seekingalpha.com/article/1333281-starbucks-more-than-just-a-coffee-shop

PURPOSE AND PROFIT

Nobel Laureate economist Milton Friedman stated[5] that the purpose of the company is to make a profit. I remember my first finance lecture at business school, (the rest is a haze …) when I was introduced to this concept.

But now I know that this doesn't work. Customers do not come to you to provide you with a profit. Customers want to see that you care about their needs, wants and expectations. It is up to leaders to align their teams to see that helping customers *earns* them a profit.

This is why purpose is externally oriented, focused on service rather than profit or sales.

5 Wikipedia, "Friedman Doctrine," last modified April 1, 2017 https://en.wikipedia. org/wiki/Friedman_ doctrine

The Royal Marines has, as an organization, the higher purpose of service to Her Majesty the Queen and to serve the United Kingdom in operations both foreign and domestic.

As part of that larger unifying purpose, I joined the Royal Marines for the sense of adventure and physical challenge. Also, I wanted to challenge myself with things that most people couldn't do, undertaking the leadership challenge, with a young man's dream of becoming a British commando, becoming part of a brotherhood and family. These personal ambitions, or personal purposes, were not in any way in conflict with those of the larger organization. This hasn't always been the case in my corporate career.

The unifying purpose that brings an organization together can help it achieve the extraordinary. But if you asked Marines, of any age or rank, *why* they do what they do, they wouldn't talk about bravery or serving the Queen; they would talk about working with mates and not letting them down.

I remember seeing one of my marines, halfway through an operation, physically sick from fear. When I asked my troop sergeant if he was OK, he gave me a knowing look that said, "Of course he will be." That young marine then picked himself up and continued with the mission. Brave? Yes, of course, but it was through the mindset of 'not letting my mates down' that continuously caused these extraordinary people to keep moving forward and continuously inspired me about service members.

I've been to lots of conferences and leadership team meetings where such a purpose is clear and compelling, and often the leader stands on stage and articulates a compassionate, awe-inspiring story about a customer or a client. Where it goes wrong is when individuals get back to their desks and the day-to-day activities and behaviours eclipse their ability to focus on their purpose.

SIMPLICITY AND CLARITY

The companies that have successfully figured this out have a clearly defined purpose that is visible every day. They tend to have only four or five values that are translated into behaviours, which, in a tangible way, bring this purpose to life. To deliver on long-term strategic priorities, it's important for any organization to be clear on what it stands for, how it works and the kind of company it wants to be.

This is behind every successful data-driven culture. A compelling vision, with a few clearly defined values, makes an organization effective.

The problem is that leaders are expected to operate in a world with a high degree of complexity, yet organizations time and again struggle to give them what they need to be successful. Essentially, what leaders need is simplicity. In fact, when leaders and teams have fewer things to focus on, they can then be most effective.

An experiment showing the value of simplicity was conducted at a market on a busy weekend. There were two stalls, and each one was selling pots of jam. At one stall, 26 different pots of jam were laid out. At the other, there were only five.

The stall with 26 pots attracted a lot of attention from passers-by. Intrigued by the vast selection, people came to look at the impressive array of jams and, as you can imagine, the crowds attracted more and more people. But the stall with only five pots on offer, with a much smaller crowd, made more sales.

Why? Customers found that it took too long to figure out what do with these 26 different jams, to find out what each of them tasted like, which one they liked best and then which one they were going to buy. Whereas customers at the stall with only five pots of jam had less to think about, a simpler and quicker decision to make, which made it easier for them to make a purchase.

I have seen first-hand business transformation teams fall down this trap time and time again; by continuously adding to the pot, they lose sight of the outcome they had set out to achieve at the start.

At a large bank in London, I was part of a cultural transformation team that was building new joiner websites, induction programmes, leadership programmes, academies, brochures, apps, you name it, all of which became small back-office science projects for leaders who were 'trying to help'. But what the organizations was really craving was clarity and simplicity so that they could focus on the important parts of their work – helping their clients and customers be successful in a volatile and turbulent economy. The result was that the organization struggled to establish stable leadership.

NATURAL CAPACITY FOR INFORMATION

Human organizations have always been based around small groups. Thousands of years ago, when humans lived in small agrarian communities, families were quite small. So the family unit was made up of four people, on average, sometimes with the grandparents.

But in those days, families coexisted in a larger group, normally in a village that was made up of around 120 people. This evolved out of the capability that humans have in maintaining numerous relationships. Of course, you can spend a lot of time maintaining multiple relationships beyond this number, but you can't get on with other stuff – a day job or whatever that may be.

For this same reason, the size of hunting groups was generally limited to about 30 men. Thirty men would go off in groups and hunt for a couple days and then return to their village.

Moving to more recent times, the first military formation designers learned from this behavioural trait and used this ideology to organize armies based on this same numeric construct. A company of soldiers was normally made up of approximately 100 to 130 people. It was broken down into four sets of 30, each making up a smaller formation – referred to today as a troop or platoon. These were then further broken down into three sections of eight men, consisting of two teams of four.

Leaders cannot get close to all the members of their teams. I recall that, throughout my military career, my strongest relationships were with my troop sergeant and my three section corporals. I allowed and encouraged each of them to build their respective teams and relationships. All I had to do was to be concerned with those four and give them all the support that they needed.

In a data-driven culture, we see a shift from the executive to the team. Organizations have evolved through a manufacturing era, where command and control and hierarchical structure were the blueprint for success. Operational excellence, controlled from the centre, worked well during this era. This does not work in the information age, when teams must feel empowered to ask questions, fail and challenge the status quo. Authority must shift towards the front line of organizations and teams, where connectivity between them is the winning advantage. I will share examples of where this works well in later chapters.

KEY CONSIDERATIONS FOR TEAMS

Align data to what's important:

- What are we seeing in our world?
- What does it mean to be great here?
- Why will people want to work with us?
- Who do we serve?
- How can we drive value for them?

Identify one key business-value driver to which we all align as a team.

Write it down.

This is where your data discovery must start.

CHAPTER 2
DATA-DRIVEN BEHAVIOURS

It is the teams and social mechanics of an organization that inform its culture. Senior leaders, of course, have to model the right behaviours, but it is through daily team interactions that this game is won and lost.

I remember being at a conference in London when the chairman of the organization stood in front of the room and said, "Culture is defined by what we don't allow." He was referring to safety, and how leaders throughout the organization need to have the courage to speak up when they see something going wrong. To me, this seems like a great perspective from which to look at how behaviour drives culture in a working group or team environment.

Another example is a very good friend of mine who has a family of four boys, all under the age of eight. As you can imagine, this makes mealtimes quite a challenging time of day. He and his wife do a fantastic job of clarifying what is and isn't allowed at the dinner table. I remember one of the boys turning to place a sausage in his brother's ear, and his mother snapped, "We don't do that around here – do we?" As I was doing my best not to chuckle, I realized that this was such a simple example of how what you do and don't allow informs the culture of any team.

On the other hand, I remember my first day of work at one of the largest banks in the United Kingdom. At the entrance to the headquarters in London, there were large signs: 'We want to be the most admired, respected, trusted … ' But the behaviours that took place under the aegis of these assertions were not seen at all. Quite the opposite occurred, as soon as you entered the elevator and made your way to your first meeting. Leaders failed to live these behaviours themselves, and internal politics and the unwillingness to share insights and knowledge permeated every meeting.

The communication of a data culture through team interactions is critical, and successful communication of what's important to act as the handrail is what you see at great companies, such as the charity I worked for and the Intercontinental Hotels group. They have values that translate into their behaviour. You see it in the way that employees in these companies interact every day.

You see this same communication in the Royal Marines. These are establishments with a very clear culture, and from the top through to the bottom, everybody can understand and translate the organization's values into a clearly defined set of behaviours.

The Royal Marines' commando tests are not about demonstrating physical ability; it's not too hard to find someone off the street who can run a certain distance or pass various types of fitness tests. The commando tests are used to identify recruits who don't exhibit the behaviours required to be part of the Royal Marines. In fact, if such individuals were to make it through both, the organization and eventually the individual could suffer. So for this reason, when I was responsible for training Royal Marine recruits, it was easy to fail someone who didn't exhibit these behaviours and values during the commando tests.

Recruiting the right individuals results in creating an organizational culture in which you know that you can trust the person next to you 100% and vice versa. Everything centres on this trust.

In the Royal Marines, the question, "What are the consequences of my actions?" is asked from day one, when recruits have to pass inspections as a team. If one member cuts corners or doesn't share information, the whole team suffers. So from the very start, Royal Marines are always thinking as a team of teams. It is deeply ingrained into the culture: "I don't want to let my team down."

A DATA-DRIVEN CULTURE

To move towards a data-driven culture, you need a set of social mechanics that will change the behaviour of people and teams tangibly every day, in meetings, in the way they interact with each other and, most important-ly, in the way they make decisions. This doesn't come from a survey, followed by a transformation map that takes three to five years to implement, but rather from manifesting simple behaviours that help people connect data to what's important to the organization.

In other words, stuff people do all the time.

The head coach of England's rugby team, Eddie Jones, who at the time of writing this book was on the cusp of breaking a world record for consecutive wins, was known by his team to give this clear and simple direction in the midst of the intense pressure of performing in an international-level sport.

At the start of the training week, prior to a game, he asked the analytics team for three things that the data told them they needed to focus on. The analytics team would distil all the data into three focused areas, such as kicking percentages of the opposition, tackle success rates or tactics during certain periods of play, and that was what the players focused on. So the young international sport stars – and thinking about the 90,000 screaming fans and millions watching on television – would have confidence in that they were looking at the right tactical areas, and confidence in the leadership and the analytics! This became a ritual for the analytics team and the way they interacted with players. Everyone was clear, and all discussions were aligned to those three important focus areas. A simple ritual fostered a data culture around clarity, and proved to result in world champions at the highest level of sport.

At Virgin Atlantic, one value is 'peace of mind'. But, what would this mean to someone who works in the maintenance department?

When the maintenance colleagues have done a good job, it means that an aircraft has been well maintained, adheres to the standards and will pass the necessary inspections to deem it suitable for flying. The team will have peace of mind that this aircraft is safe.

For colleagues in operations and scheduling, it means that they will deliver this aircraft back into the fleet when promised. This also provides peace of mind.

And for the cabin crew, it's about providing peace of mind to customers during the flight. If a seat is wobbly, and a passenger is uncomfortable, the cabin crew takes steps to fix it or come up with another solution.

Behaviours, informed by values, need to work everywhere in the organization and they need to lead to tangible action, rather than to some lofty aspiration of where the company wants to go. It is through this lens that I'd like to share with you the behaviours an organization needs to display in order to become data-driven, to use data and advanced skill sets to explore new areas of opportunity.

Here is where the true value of data can be realized.

*Your organization has patterns of thinking
and behaving which are encouraged
or discouraged. THAT is your culture.*

Carolyn Taylor
Author, *Walking the Talk*

DATA-DRIVEN MINDSET

How can organizations help their leaders move into the information age effectively?

How can they help leaders shape the right behaviours and teams to become more data driven?

How can the critical gap between domain and analytics skills be closed?

This mindset challenge has nothing to do with technology or data, but rather involves building the right behaviours in teams so that we shift from a manufacturing mindset to a data-driven mindset see Figure 3.

FIGURE 3: TEAM DATA-DRIVEN MIND-SET SHIFT

FROM	TO
This is what happened yesterday …	What's going to happen tomorrow?
This is what I need to do …	This is what I need to know
Long-range planning …	Picture what could be
Scenario planning …	Iterate, challenge and debate
Internal focus …	External orientation

After more than eight years of research, I have identified the seven behavioural traits that – when combined with a clear and compelling purpose – drive daily actions to create the direction for any organization that wishes to build a data-driven culture.

#1 ⚛ ALIGN DATA COLLECTION TO PURPOSE

As discussed earlier, leaders need to live their purpose every day through the decisions that they make for their organizations' significant others – their customers, clients, members or patients. But more importantly in the data age, they need to create a line of sight between this purpose and data collection. In other words, the advanced analytical skills that they have access to should be guided by their purpose as a handrail for exploration.

This will enable leaders to then drive structured questioning using consistent, simple language that helps to connect analytics to upcoming opportunities and aspirations.

Finally, the insights derived from the analysis need to be combined with the experience of leaders and teams.

Decisions need to be made based on a combination of experience *and* data-derived insights, with purpose always as the handrail for discussion – a guiding light.

Example:

I worked for a retail client in North America recently and, at their strategy launch event, the CEO stood up on stage and went through some well-crafted slides that outlined in detail their Aspiration, Vision, Strategic Imperative and Must-Win Battles. As I sat in the crowd among the leaders who were tasked with delivering this grand plan, I could sense that they were lost as to what the handrail for discovery was. What were the words that were going to guide them in the daily questions needed to ask to from the data?

As I will discuss in later chapters, teams need to build an ambidextrous skill. This is the ability to execute a plan while exploring for new opportunities using data, with clarity around what's important acting as the glue that unites both these aspects. This is why the behavioural trait of leaders to align data collection to purpose is so important in the data age for teams.

The guide for exploration must be purpose, as it is this that stands true over time. The plan and vision will change as teams change, as will strategic goals and must-win battles (blah, blah, blah) but the people you serve won't. If organizations seek to build an enduring and ever-building data ecosystem – in other words, a deeper understanding of what the customers are going to want next – then the framework for this must not change with new leadership teams and must remain consistent in every corner of the organization. Leadership teams that continuously move this goalpost will not survive in the data age. Those that use it as a benchmark for exploration and data discovery will win, as they start to develop a deep level of foresight on what matters – their purpose and the reason they exist.

This retailer's purpose was about building trust in the neighbourhoods that they served. Using this as the focus for every leader to ask questions of the data, from the front line to the centre, would have been industry-leading and would have led to the strategic foresight that they were seeking.

It was, after all, a battle with a big competitor: their competitor was Amazon!

Instead, the data team (and CDO) was kept close to the CEO and data discovery was kept close to the central 'plan'. So leaders in the organization received sales data reports or, as one regional manager told me, "We were given our newspaper and told how to read it." The irony was that the responsibility for their proximity to the neighbourhoods that they served, and the purpose, lay with the front-line teams where this behaviour was needed most to win.

KEY TAKEAWAY

Every leader needs to clearly articulate to their teams why the organization exists. This isn't a generic goal-setting exercise cascaded from top management, but the responsibility of each leader of every team, doing so in a way that energizes their teams to use purpose as a guide for data collection.

#2
CHAMPION DATA EXPLOITATION

Leaders need to build the right skills to query data rather than requesting 'data reports'.

For years we have mastered building annual plans and populating tasks and goals into spreadsheets or software. The notion that 'you can't manage what you can't measure' *no longer holds true*. Now, leaders need to master the skill of asking questions, seeking support from data skill sets at every juncture in a highly iterative way.

They need to promote the translation of data and the sharing of insights across the entire organization. Too often, data and information are used as a means to wield power and kept closely to the 'owners' of such insights for political gain.

But, winning organizations are those that purvey insights to those who need to know them, irrespective of functional siloes or politics. Here is where best practices can be exploited.

Example:

A consumer packaged goods (CPG) client that I worked with recently had gone through a series of restructuring phases that were handled by a management consultancy as they sought to 'get closer to customers'. What followed was a confusing re-organization, in which team responsibilities were rearranged and new team titles were given.

This resulted in exactly the wrong type of behaviour for data exploitation. "I'm not responsible for that area … no longer me" was the response given when asked a question by another team. With the best intent, teams were focused on their new areas of responsibility and it was an unintentional exacerbation of siloed thinking.

Unfortunately, the strategic centre adopted sharing by stealing and replicating good ideas through staged conference calls on a weekly basis. Instead of sharing insights that each respective regional team had discovered through its own analysis, the conversations on these calls usually involved complaining about tasks from the top, complaining about the lack of or inefficient use of resources and the familiar comical corporate conference calls where people 'come and go'. The teams needed to move from 'managing upwards' towards translating and sharing insights.

In a data-exploitation environment, leaders conduct a level of analysis and interpretation of data locally and then commit to sharing this with 'those who need to know'. This is an unshakable commitment to translate insights consistently by using a common language. The strategic centre can then exploit these insights by pushing them to teams elsewhere and, by doing so, start to build their own level of understanding of what is going on throughout the organization.

This should have nothing to do with the title or position of the teams involved, but rather a commitment to sharing and exploiting the power of the network. Here, the power of the organization and data can be truly harnessed.

CASE STUDY – WALMART

STAYING AHEAD OF 260 MILLION CUSTOMERS

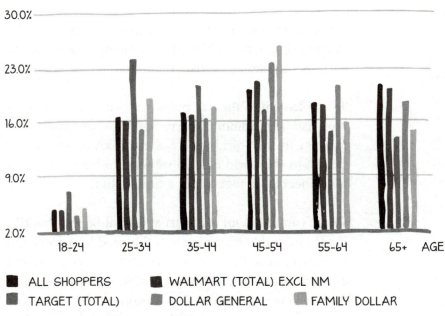

Age Breakdown of US Walmart Shoppers – Source: Kantar[6]

Legend:
- ALL SHOPPERS
- WALMART (TOTAL) EXCL NM
- TARGET (TOTAL)
- DOLLAR GENERAL
- FAMILY DOLLAR

We've seen that, in today's markets, getting ahead of the customer is critical to success. In retail, which is one of the toughest markets in the world, unless customers find what they want, when they want it and at the price they want, they look elsewhere. And this applies to both purchases online and in physical stores.

6 Kantar Report, "Building an Insights Engine," Kantar website, Nov. 26, 2016, last accessed on August 25, 2017 http://us.kantar.com/business/brands/2016/building-an-insights-engine/

Walmart is the largest retailer in the United States, with globally more than 11,000 stores, 260 million customers and 2.3 million employees. They successfully made $473 billion in sales in 2016.

Few retailers have as broad a spectrum, in terms of their customer demographics, as Walmart does. Walmart customers are from low-to-middle-income demographic groups, but in addition to this group, they also attract college students, single parents and large families.

Yet, despite the vast differences in their customer demographic groups, Walmart is regularly able to define customer wishes and satisfy them well.

To implement Walmart's purpose, former CEO Bill Simon had large ambitions: "We want to know what every product in the world is. We want to know who every person in the world is. And we want to have the ability to connect them together in a transaction."

Simon's ambition for Walmart and what he was describing through this statement was the need to understand customers in different countries, different cultures and different markets across the world. By being able to predict various key areas such as customer needs, pains or budgets, the teams across Walmart would have the information they required to fulfil Simon's ambition.

Walmart is able to do this because they have the skills and resources to collect data with supreme efficiency. In fact, Walmart boasts the largest data hub in the world, called the 'Data Café'. This is a state-of-the-art analytics hub located within its Bentonville, Arkansas headquarters. Café actually stands for Collaborative Analytics Facilities for Enterprise. In the Data Café, more than

200 streams of internal and external data, including 40 petabytes of recent transactional data, can be modelled, manipulated, visualized and connected to the leadership community.[7]

But, aside from collecting large amounts of data, you will recall, as discussed earlier, that organizations that succeed are those that utilize data and have a heightened level of *understanding* from data.

Walmart is not only skilled at collecting data, the company has also created a data-driven culture. Teams from the front lines take their business questions and issues to the analytics experts for analysis. Together, insights from the front line and the data analytics provide valuable information that is shared across the company. The leadership also utilizes this information to drive the direction of the company on the whole.

Walmart's Senior Statistical Analyst, Naveen Peddamail, said, "If you can't get insights until you've analysed your sales for a week or a month, then you've lost sales within that time. If you can cut down that time of two or three weeks to 20 or 30 minutes, then that saves a lot of money for Walmart and stops us from losing sales. That's the real value of what we have built with the Data Café."

7 Bernard Marr, "Really Big Data at Walmart," Forbes, January 23, 2017, last accessed August 25, 2017 https://www.forbes.com/sites/bernardmarr/2017/01/23/really-big-data-at-walmart-real-time-insights-from-their-40-petabyte-data-cloud/#6e04cc906c10

Innovation happens at the edges …
not at the top.

Simon Sinek
Author, *Start With Why*

A classic example is Walmart's US food sales. Teams on the south coast of the US were having trouble selling Pop Tarts® – a kind of breakfast pastry. They took the problem to the data analysts team, who found that sales of Pop Tarts® increased sharply before a hurricane. They concluded that consumers bought Pop Tarts® prior to a hurricane because they could be stored and made easily when they would essentially be locked up at home. By the simple action of moving the Pop Tarts® to the front of stores before a hurricane, they achieved a 7% increase in its sales. Then the leaders tried the same tactic at stores in other regions, which were less threatened by hurricanes, but suffered other types of weather challenges, and found similar success.

Multiply this kind of insight by tens of thousands, and it's easy to see how Walmart succeeds in anticipating its customers' requirements.

ASKING DATA BETTER QUESTIONS

Essentially, for Walmart, it is a question of getting the right products to the right locations – in front of the right customers – at the right time, at the right price. Consumers keep coming back to the stores when they find what they are looking for, so Walmart must know what their customers want before they come.

At Walmart, questions are received by the data analysis team from both leaders and the front lines. Leaders contribute a broader perspective, as they have knowledge of the market in which they operate and of the company as a whole. Whereas, those in the front line have knowledge on particular issues that arise: Why is a given product not selling? Should we stock a certain product ahead of a holiday? And so on. Insights derived from the data, therefore, include input from all across the organization.

Using their Data Cafés, Walmart tracks consumers on an individual basis – Walmart has exhaustive customer data on close to 145 million Americans.[8] Consumer trend insights are gathered on what products are in favour, in what regions, and what price ranges are accessible to them. The company also tracks what is trending on social media and takes note of local events, such as a major sports competition. As we've seen, weather changes are tracked to see how they affect buying patterns. All the events are captured and analysed intelligently by big-data algorithms.

In many ways, the procedures used by Walmart are very like those used by the military when it applies the techniques of activity-based intelligence to derive insights from large masses of unstructured data. Faced with the need to anticipate hostile activity amid a complex, changing and inchoate landscape, the data scientists try to understand the unknown by finding patterns of activity.

8 Jillian Berman, "Walmart now possesses info on 145 million Americans," Huffington Post, November 26, 2013, last accessed August 25, 2017 http://www.huffingtonpost.com/2013/11/26/walmart-data_n_4344879.html

ACTING LIKE A NETWORK

9 Jessica Lombardo, Walmart Organizational Structure and Culture, Panmore Institute, January 17, 2017, last accessed August 25, 2017 http://panmore.com/walmart-organizational-structure-organizational-culture

10 Walmart website, last modified; not available http://corporate.walmart.com/newsroom/company-facts

On one hand, Walmart maintains the traditional structure of workers reporting to managers.[9]

On the other hand, the company has created a network among its 2.3 million associates[10] who drive Walmart's stores, e-commerce business, logistics and other functions through sharing information crucial to serving customers better.

Walmart's leaders believe all associates have an important voice and play a critical role in driving business. Sam Walton, the founder of Walmart, is often quoted as saying, "Listen to your associates, they're your best idea generators." The company believes that any of its associates may come up with the next big idea that will continue to separate Walmart from its competitors. This thinking connects employees on the front lines and those involved in other aspects of operations into a network. This thinking creates the right framework of questions to be asked of data gathered and supports discussion and implementation of insights derived from data.[11]

To encourage and facilitate this, teams from any part of the business are invited to the Data café, where they can discuss problems with the analysts and work with them to devise solutions.

The organization's ability to work and succeed with this sharing and its data-driven culture is a tribute to the leadership that has fostered a data-driven culture at every level of Walmart.

11 Glassdoor Team, "How Walmart builds its corporate culture," Glassdoor website, October 28, 2016, last accessed August 25, 2017 https://www. glassdoor.com/ employers/blog/learn- best-walmart-builds- corporate-culture/

KEY TAKEAWAY

Every leader must commit to the network. This means sharing the insights that they discover with those who need to know. This leadership behaviour is more than just firing out emails with attachments, but thinking through where this insight can add most value to the wider team.

_____

_____

_____

_____

_____

_____

#3 DEMAND-PREDICTIVE ANALYTICS

Leaders need to have a sure view of today's and tomorrow's trends and opportunities. Not just a reference to the past, but a secure grasp of what is happening today and what will happen tomorrow – a predictive mindset towards data is the key.

What are my customers' future needs, pains and pinch points?

By looking forward using predictive analytics, leaders can build an inquisitive environment for their teams. This can be achieved by adding simple rudimentary techniques that may be lacking in some levels in organizations, such as 'what-if' analysis and war gaming, in which teams test, iterate and learn through data. These are skills that need to be built and applied every day, in meetings and leadership interactions to challenge *everyday* bias – and not just during a two-day team event offsite in a hotel somewhere.

Keep this simple. Predictive analytics require a highly advanced analytical skill set to handle complex data. But competitive advantage can be found immediately with business teams who start to adopt the behaviour of looking forward using analytics and asking such forward-looking questions.

Example:

The simple, 0:20:80 principle was instilled into all military intelligence professionals working with front-line teams on day one of their training (see Figure 4 below).

FIGURE 4: 0:20:80 PRINCIPLE

YESTERDAY TODAY TOMORROW

0 : 20 : 80

Using the 0:20:80 principle:

- 0% of analysis looks at what happened yesterday
- 20% of analysis looks at what is happening today
- 80% of analysis looks at what is going to happen tomorrow

This is a mindset, not a framework.

In other words, of course teams will and should refer to yesterday's data, but the majority of the analysis, discussion and focus needs to be on "What is going to happen tomorrow?" Here are some questions worth considering:

- ☐ What are our clients going to be asking from us?
- ☐ What are our customers going to be buying?
- ☐ What are the health needs of our patients going to be?

This may sound like a market research activity, but successfully instilling this thinking and behaviour in every team will result in a successful data-driven organization. Additionally, you can appreciate how happy marketeers would be if front-line teams shared these insights with them.

KEY TAKEAWAY

Through a subtle, but critically important, behavioural change of always pushing towards tomorrow, organizations can successfully move away from "What needs to be to succeed in a plan" to "What needs to be known to achieve (future) customer value."

_____

_____

_____

_____

_____

_____

_____

#4 EMPOWER OTHERS TO ACT

Leaders need to champion the use of data-driven decision-making at all levels of the organization.

If organizations don't use scale to their advantage and share the best practices of where data has been used to achieve business value, they will fall short, as illustrated by the example of the team I led in Afghanistan at the beginning of this book. Here is where they can compete with the smaller 'disruptors' in their industries.

Leaders need to embed the capability for idea generation through data at all levels of the organization, and to decentralize authority in decision-making.

Data-confident talent is needed at the front line and they should be empowered to ask the right questions of the data and lead the organization to understanding their customers better.

Example:

Mission Command is a leadership principle that has been adopted by the US and British military forces over the last 30 years. It refers to aligning teams to the strategic intent through articulating the 'why' of a mission or goal, combined with the 'what' of the mission.

The 'what and why' form a powerful tool for leaders in the data age. As we seek to democratize analytics and put business intelligence and analytics tools into the hands of end users, leadership teams will need to master the balance between autonomy and alignment. The 'why' and strategic context will guide the interaction of domain and analytics teams. The 'what' relates to clarity of the task at hand and the details of what needs be done.

KEY TAKEAWAY

Give your teams the direction and let them go. This is hands-off leadership, in which your teams know where you are if they need you, but have the freedom and confidence to discover within safe boundaries.

#5 PROMOTE ACCESS TO DATA FOR ALL

In a secure way, all leaders must ensure that access to a single source of truth for business value-adding data is made available to all teams throughout the organization.

The chief data officer should act as the interface between the business and the principal adviser on where data can add the most value, building confidence in teams to access data. In the case of Walmart and their Data Café, we can think of the business leaders as the customers and data scientists as the baristas serving coffee!

The British military intelligence community went through a significant cultural shift with this over the past 15 years, too.

Our intelligence efforts were but a cottage industry compared to the American fusion machine and use of databases. When we compare what we had in Iraq with what we had in Northern Ireland, we could see what we were lacking. We need to deploy on campaigns with a database that will allow us to fuse, analyse and exploit intelligence and historical data in order to act as a tool for commanders, rather than as merely a TOP SECRET filing cabinet.

Divisional COS- Iraq 2008[12]

12 British Army Field Manual: Counter Insurgency Operations, last modified November 16, 2009 news.bbc.co.uk/1/ shared/bsp/hi/ pdfs/16_11_09_ army_manual.pdf

KEY TAKEAWAY

Organizations don't know what they already know. Data silos are the enemy of a data culture and it's a leadership responsibility to promote access to data for the team. Technology is no longer an excuse; the final mile here is leadership behaviour and a commitment to transparency.

_____

_____

_____

_____

_____

_____

#6
CONNECT DATA TALENT TO BUSINESS CONTEXT

With all the hype and excitement surrounding big data, business leaders and their teams are struggling to find where they should start in gathering and utilizing data. Data has no value unless it's linked to a business metric.

All data and business leaders should be seeking clarity on what the business team is trying to achieve and where data can add the most value. Providing clarity as a strategic objective is of critical importance to advance analytical skills and to build data-driven teams. Nowadays, analytics are no longer only a concern for the information technology function or other technical functions. Analytics are now a part of new types of teams and the behaviour of the leaders of these teams supports its interaction. Data analysts must be comfortable with asking 'stupid questions' around the domain context – irrespective of number of PhDs!

Business teams possess the skills and experience to know where value creation is needed – after all, they know their products, customers and markets better than anyone. The key behaviour that business teams need today is to take what are often well-thought-out Key Performance Indicators and set big data on the right path to explore these further.

As business leaders, we have been working with small data for decades – it's *this* data that helps us achieve business goals every day. Teams periodically plan and assess long-term strategy, setting and resetting strategic goals – but what are the metrics, or small data, that matter day-to-day?

- *Grow e-commerce sales by 34% to achieve $142million*
- *Europe the Middle East and Africa to deliver $1.7bn in sales*
- *Deliver $33m in supply chain savings*
- *Deliver $429m in sales from projects (growth of 10%)*
- *Efficiency savings $12.5M*

Big data examples are everywhere, including analysis from social media data, mobile phone GPS data, data from sensors in street lamps, bus stops and cars. All these create a huge amount of data sets, and only successful teams will have the ability to link the metrics that matter to further explore the data.

KEY TAKEAWAY

Business leaders must ensure that the data talent they adopt into their teams have a full understanding of the business context – what matters most to the team and why. They must create an environment where this talent feels safe to challenge assumptions and check bias and groupthink. Only then will teams unlock the true potential of this resource.

#7 ⬡ BUILD A SHARED UNDERSTANDING

Leaders must commit to placing understanding at the centre of everything they do and the questions they ask. Questioning data, and discussions and planning with data skills should all have the purpose of enhancing a team's understanding of what is important. This is again linked to 'purpose'.

Although we often hear that 'knowledge is power', it is important to note that in today's world, almost all organizations have access to vast quantities of information. So, the defining behaviour of an organization's teams is how they combine this with analysis and judgment to derive the right insight and then make the right decisions.

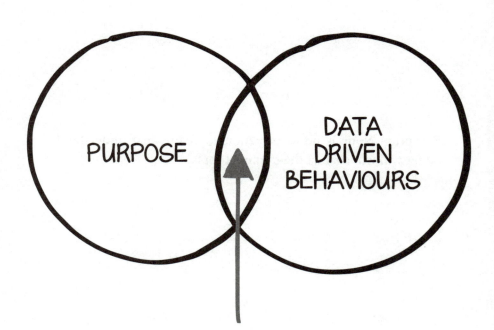

INTRODUCTION

PART ONE

CHAPTER 1

CHAPTER 2

CHAPTER 3

CHAPTER 4

PART TWO

CHAPTER 5

CHAPTER 6

CHAPTER 7

PART THREE

CHAPTER 8

CHAPTER 9

CHAPTER 10

CONCLUSION

KEY TAKEAWAY

Execution alone is no longer enough. Teams that understand better will win against their competitors.

_____

_____

_____

_____

_____

_____

_____

_____

_____

KEY CONSIDERATIONS FOR TEAMS

Build seven data-driven behaviours into your team:

1. Align data collection to purpose
2. Champion data exploitation
3. Demand predictive analytics
4. Empower others to act
5. Promote access to data for all
6. Connect data exploration to business context
7. Build a shared understanding

Encouraging or discouraging these behaviours will mean the difference in your data culture journey.

CHAPTER 3
DISCOVERY

To find out what the future must be,
you must create it.

Steve Jobs
Founder, Apple

Organizations need to operate at the intersection of data-driven behaviours and their purpose. Where these two meet, leaders and teams throughout the organization need to build a discovery-driven mindset. Having this mindset will ensure that they are constantly asking data the right questions, the answers of which will lead them to discover new areas of growth and opportunities as they continue to be guided by what matters most – purpose.

The insights gained from data must be shared, and used to inform the entire organization. This does not imply a senior marketing team asking more questions, but rather ensuring that these individuals are better connected with the front-line teams that are asking questions and being curious every day. As we democratize data and analytics through technology, this sharing and connection of knowledge will create a competitive advantage for teams in every industry.

CASE STUDY – KODAK

FROM RESTRUCTURING TO SUCCESS WITH FORESIGHT

(Note: Kodak Alaris is a spin-off from the company that does big-data analysis and scanners – it is no longer related in any way to Eastman Kodak.)

Kodak has become the poster-child for failing to adapt to disruption. Everyone knows that Kodak nearly went bankrupt because it didn't take digital photography seriously, even though the company had been one of the early pioneers of the technology.

But since it came out of restructuring in September 2013, Kodak has taken to trend analysis via data analytics and begun building products ahead of customer trends, employing the foresight it so sadly lacked in the past.

"We collect data via mobile apps, email marketing, and Customer Relationship Management and that is useful for making particular business decisions," points out Kodak Chief Marketing Officer Steven Overman.[13]

But Overman places equal emphasis on situational awareness, which was also heavily lacking in Kodak's past. "But let us not forget to just open our eyes and ears, engage in conversation and see what's all around us."[14]

Back in 2000, Kodak had been in existence for nearly 120 years and defined its purpose in terms of past trends. At that time, Kodak was all about the film and the paper and the chemicals. Kodak's mindset was inwardly focused; they talked about "people take pictures using a normal camera, on a normal roll of film and then have a developer print them on paper." It was based on what Kodak did, not on what consumers wanted.

If Kodak had stuck to their original purpose – 'sharing memories' – then they could have exploited their early invention of the digital camera successfully. 'How' people shared memories didn't seem to matter to Kodak, whereas great companies can take their core purpose and direct it into new realms. Kodak saw the new digital technology as a disruption to their core business, rather than an opportunity to adapt. They chose to continue with their old, secure business of non-digitally 'sharing memories', but then found that their competitors were fast embracing digital technology successfully.

The culture needed to change at Kodak, and CMO Steven Overman explains how. For Overman, the most important CMO attribute is curiosity. "We have to be agile and willing to learn," he says. "We are at the forefront of change – the toolbox at our disposal in terms of channels is changing all the time. That pace of change won't slow down or stop. And in terms of data proliferation,

13 Nadia Cameron, "CMO Interview," cmo.com, October 24, 2016, last accessed August 25, 2017 https://www. cmo.com.au/ article/608998/ cmo-interview-part-2-what-it-takes-lead-kodak-marketing-function/

14 Ibid

we are going to have to decide what data is useful and what isn't. That requires an ability to learn."

Overman says the cultural transformation of Kodak is as important as the renewal of the brand externally.

"People at Kodak are incredibly resilient, but they had been traumatized," he says of the staff culture he stepped into two years earlier. "Going through Chapter 11 almost feels amoral. You suddenly can't and don't have to pay people you love and rely on. The majority of employees were there through that experience and there was a lot of latent shame associated with it. What unified everybody was a hunger to thrive and prove they could change," Overman says.

But culture doesn't change just because the CMO or CEO says it should, Overman points out. "Culture is what happens in the every day – in the way we make decisions, communicate with each other," he says. To make these changes, Kodak took specific actions, like distributing the executive leadership team globally, and Overman is based in London rather than New York, with colleagues in Singapore and San Francisco.

"It indicates the need to work better remotely and virtually, and how we need to apply learnings from different sociocultural environments into the way we operate," Overman says.

The same way that the new night convoy tactics in Afghanistan were shared to me from a different team from a different location and country – driven by a data insight.

In 2013, the company took a hard look at the market for the services in which it still had an edge. They accessed insight derived from data to see where opportunities existed for assets the company already had. Digital printing was one; film and coating technology was another. A major effort was made to develop foresight, anticipating business-to-business and consumer trends and targeting those already in motion.

Kodak then leveraged its existing assets to target those trends.

"Stripped to its basics, the company has always been one of the world's foremost experts at coating. It became a household name by layering a plastic base with light-sensitive chemicals and selling it in little yellow boxes by the billions. Essentially, Kodak's plan for survival is to continue putting stuff atop other stuff," explains Communications Daily analyst Matthew Daneman.[15]

That includes printing and 3D printing and then more specialist technologies, such as atomic layer research, bonding microscopically thin materials to surfaces.

Analytics is now a key part of its print offering. The Kodak Prinergy Cloud, an analytics-enabled cloud platform, offers print service providers (PSPs) new industry-first solutions to minimize both cost and risk while at the same time driving business growth.

To meet demands, Kodak is collaborating with other companies to produce smaller and more innovative

15 Mathew Daneman, "Kodak Next," Democrat and Chronicle, September 1, 2013, last accessed August 25, 2017 http://media. democratandchronicle. com/kodaknext/pdf/ KodakNext.pdf

sensors as the Internet of Things continues to develop. And the company is seeking to turn semiconductor production on its head, by researching solutions for printing them onto circuit boards instead of going through the laborious cleaning-room process.

Kodak has also very effectively diversified geographically, with a footprint in more than 150 countries, as insights from the global printing market data analysis made it clear where opportunities were to be found. A large percentage of revenue now comes from emerging markets. The global operation generated $1 billion in revenue in 2016, and it helped the company turn its first annual profit – a modest $16 million – since filing for bankruptcy in 2012.[16]

With its eye on new consumer demographics – millennials – Kodak has joined forces with hip designers Opening Ceremony to produce a fashion line, where Kodak prints photos on shirts for designers Carol Lim and Humberto Leon.

Again, seeking to stay ahead of consumer trends, Kodak came out with a smartphone in 2015 – one that was more camera than phone. It did not get good reviews in the technical press, but it's an important start that the company can build on.

16 "Kodak Reports Net Earnings for 2016 of $16 Million," Kodak website, last modified; not available http://www.kodak.com/us/en/corp/press_center/kodak_reports_net_earnings_for_2016_of_16_million/default.htm

BEWARE OF THE "PLAN"!

From first-hand experience, I am more than aware of how traditional planning cycles stifle discovery and curiosity. I was working with a senior leadership team that had been focused on strategy execution for 18 months following a global acquisition. When I asked them, "What next?" during a planning session, I was greeted with a room full of blank faces. By focusing on executing the plan, alignment and frankly, a bureaucratic and slow cascade to ensure that everyone 'was on the same page', they had shot themselves in the foot and destroyed all hope of future innovations into the future. The team felt like the convoy that I led years before: big, slow and vulnerable to attack from the smallest target at any point. All they relied on was efficiency to react if required!

*Hierarchical, command-and-control
approaches don't work anymore.
They impede information flows inside companies,
hampering the fluid and collaborative
nature of work today.*

Louis V. Gerstner,
Former CEO of IBM

*"… landing a man on the moon and
returning him safely to earth
in the next decade …"*

John F. Kennedy

I've lost count of the number of times that I've heard the statement opposite being used to galvanize teams around a long-term strategic objective. Don't get me wrong, this is a powerful and compelling set of words that draws everybody's attention to what needs to be achieved. It provides a goal for all teams to rally behind and to gauge their everyday work and execution.

However, the idea of setting out a five-year strategic plan needs to be 'balanced' with behaviours in the volatile and uncertain environments in which many organizations now operate. We know that disruption can come from anywhere; examples such as Uber, Airbnb, Alibaba and the craft beer revolution have all demonstrated that the largest and most resilient of organizations and brands that are too focused on a set plan will die.

As with the 1.5km long, slow-moving convoy that was vulnerable to an attack as I led it through an extremely volatile city with all sorts of complexities, such organizations are being subjected to 'death by a thousand cuts', with start-ups weaving in and out of their markets, fearless and with nothing to lose.

The mortality rate of organizations is higher than it's ever been. Public companies are perishing much earlier in their life spans than ever before. Almost one-tenth of all public companies fail each year, a fourfold increase since 1965.[17]

17 BCG Report, "Die Another Day: What Leaders Can Do About the Shrinking Life Expectancy of Corporations," BCG website, December 2, 2015, last accessed August 25, 2017 https://www.bcgperspectives.com/content/articles/strategic-planning-growth-die-another-day/

Take the case of retail chain Whole Foods. In June 2017, Amazon announced that it will acquire Whole Foods Market, a grocery chain with more than 450 retail stores, for $13.7 billion. Amazon's stock price rose 2.4%, but at the same time, the stock price of competing retailers like SuperValu, Kroger and Sprouts fell sharply. This was clearly a game changer for food retailers, and nearly every other traditional retailer.

Amazon has turned the traditional retail game plan on its head. Instead of starting out with bricks-and-mortar stores, and then layering the digital experience on top of that, Amazon brings super-sophisticated digital experience and integrates the physical store. Clearly no retailer, online or on the ground, can escape the disruption that Amazon has created in the industry.

No retailer, and in fact no business of any kind today, is safe from such disruption. This means that organizations must change the planning and management mindsets in place, born out of a more stable environment. They need situational awareness, to stay ahead and compete disruption like that of Amazon. Teams have to constantly seek new answers, and leaders have to be driven by discovery. Organizations need to be able 'to see around corners'.

A NEW LEADERSHIP ORIENTATION

This is important when we think about what we ask our leaders to do in organizations. I remember numerous off-site sessions with leadership teams, when leaders would stand up on the first day and set out their annual goals. This was usually a great start for the team, as they galvanized around the compelling vision and challenge set before them.

What goes wrong is the bureaucratic process that follows: team members receive their goal for that year, which is then broken down into six further tasks, which are then broken down into more goals and tasks for their teams. I have seen leaders literally leave this exercise with more than 20 goals and tasks that they then take to their team, and this is where the anarchy and confusion starts, as they start to drift away from their purpose towards the distractions of dashboards and task-setting.

Control leads to compliance;
autonomy leads to engagement.

Daniel H. Pink
Author, *Drive*

Leaders have to become more exploratory and discovery-driven. But if we ask them to focus too much on the 'plan', then we would simply be killing the opportunity for discovery. And all the data in the world will matter very little.

Traditional planning, as outlined above, worked well in the stable and predictable environments of yesteryear. Back then, leaders could articulate a five-year vision, a series of annual plans and respective goals, and that was all. Today, things change too quickly to rely on that kind of planning.

Instead, we need to constantly adapt the plan, asking questions of the data, in order to identify what we need to do next.

This allows teams to improvise. But within organizations, this is still not being done well enough – there is too much of the industrial-age, manufacturing-era thinking. Leaders and teams need to follow the direction of their vision using purpose as a handrail. It's a step, it's an experiment and leaders must learn and adapt.

This is a sea change from what most leaders are doing. Responses from a recent Boston Consultancy Group survey of 120 companies around the world in 10 major industry sectors showed that executives are well aware of the need to match their strategy-making processes to the specific demands of their competitive environments. Still, the survey found, in practice, many rely instead on approaches that are better suited to predictable, stable environments, even when their own environments are known to be highly volatile or mutable. Only one in four executives surveyed was prepared to adapt to unforeseeable events.[18]

18 Martin Reeves Claire Love Philipp Tillmanns, "Your strategy needs a strategy," Harvard Business Review, September 2012 https://hbr.org/2012/09/your-strategy-needs-a-strategy

Linear planning isn't suitable for today's volatile world. The closer you come to the horizon of uncertainty, the more leaders need to become more exploratory. Traditional scenario planning, using the classic tools that we all learned at business school, such as Porter's five forces analysis or the Boston matrix model, which are based on assumptions of stability and predictability in the 1970s, are less suitable. Everything is changing at such a rapid rate nowadays that the only way to stay informed is through the use of analytical tools in an iterative and interactive way. In this way, we can identify a number of plausible scenarios for the future and stay ahead of competitors.

Once teams have established a plausible future, they can then ask how to work back from there to where they are now. All this thinking should be informed by purpose – purpose drives discovery and leads to useful questions.

KEY CONSIDERATIONS FOR TEAMS

1. Organizations need to operate at the intersection of data-driven behaviours and their purpose.
2. Build the culture to ensure teams are constantly asking data the right questions, the answers to which will lead them to discover new areas of growth.
3. Traditional planning cycles stifle discovery and curiosity.
4. Leaders have to become more exploratory and discovery-driven. If we ask them to focus too much on the 'plan', then we will kill the opportunity for discovery. And all the data in the world will matter very little.

CHAPTER 4
BUILDING A CULTURE OF UNDERSTANDING

Great leaders today are able to align people around a sense of purpose and values and get that consistency all around the globe and then empower other people to step up and lead.

Bill George
Former Chairman and CEO, Medtronic

UNDERSTANDING IN COMPLEXITY

The military intelligence community went through significant changes when faced with the complexity of 'the war on terror' from 2001 and beyond.

The biggest change was required from teams and analysts who were now asked to view the environment through a holistic lens. Conventional military practice called for thinking based on three colour-coded data categories. The enemy (Red – enemies and any other 'bad guys'), the local population (White – neutral) and the host nation forces (Blue – supportive). See Figure 5.

FIGURE 5: GOOD GUYS, BAD GUYS AND CIVILIANS' FRAMEWORK

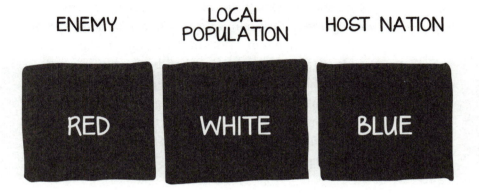

This framework was borne out of previous conflicts, when there was a clearer delineation between the enemy and other elements of society. When I was trained as an intelligence officer, our training material came from the Cold War era. This had a strong bias towards collecting data about the enemy, rather than analysing and gaining a deep understanding of the society of which the enemy was a part.

However, the analysis that emerged from this model often painted an overly simplistic intelligence picture. It failed to take sociocultural, environmental, economic and historic factors into account, and these proved to be paramount to these operations. Underestimation of the importance of this analysis came from the traditional method of focusing on enemy forces, in the most limited sense. This led to the inaccurate assumption that the enemy and the society around it were separate constructs, a separate subsystem within a larger societal system. Whereas the conflicts in Iraq and Afghanistan showed us that this type of analysis had become outmoded. In this hostile and chaotic environment, members of the local population changed their allegiances in a heartbeat. They could easily be supporting the government, then siding with the insurgency and, at the same time, end up resenting them both.

The traditional military model of using colour-coded categories failed to work here. Allegiances were constantly changing and the model consequently failed to provide decision makers with a contextual understanding of the people and groups in this environment.

For example, there were well-reported cases of an Afghan police officer or army officer entering a base that was co-located with British troops and opening fire on British troops, who were under the false sense of being protected. These seemingly friendly officers had, in fact, been radicalized or coerced in some way by a 'red' force.

It was clear that blue-labelled friends weren't, at times, necessarily friends at all. Yet, they were also not necessarily enemies. In conclusion, it was clear that more cultural factors had to be understood to analyse this complex environment.

What was required here was a new approach to data collection, and it has taken a considerable effort at evolution for the military to find a way to look at the world through a holistic lens – an officer currently training at

West Point informed me that today officer cadets take part in projects and exercises with diverse communities in Manhattan – to expose them to such societal complexities early in their careers.

In the military, leaders need to both shape the data-collection process and analyse it for decision-making. Their thinking must be broad and holistic to prevent siloed thinking from the start. After all, the primary purpose of any data analysis is to support decision-making.

A SYSTEM OF SYSTEMS

The shift in the military's approach to intelligence really started during 'Operation Enduring Freedom' (October 2001 to December 2014).

The reason for this fundamental shift in Afghanistan occurred as the demand for bottom-up insights from the front line and top-down direction from the executives of the organization increased. In January 2010, US Army Lieutenant General (ret.) Michael T. Flynn reported:

"Having focused the overwhelming majority of its collection efforts and analytical brainpower on insurgent groups, the vast intelligence apparatus is unable to answer fundamental questions about the environment in which the United States and allied forces operate and the people they seek to persuade. Ignorant of local economics and landowners, hazy about who the powerbrokers are and how they might be influenced, incurious about the correlations between various development projects and the levels of cooperation among villagers, and disengaged from people in the best position to find answers – whether aid workers or Afghan soldiers – (US) intelligence officers and analysts can do little but shrug in response to high-level decision makers seeking the knowledge analysis and information they need to wage successful counterinsurgency."

But there were cultural obstacles that had to be overcome in order for strategists to take up this new concept. The cultural bias towards focusing on 'red' enemy analysis was hard to eradicate.

This is because enemy-focused intelligence efforts offer a tangible reward for intelligence officers and their teams. Enemy intelligence feeds often lead directly to the capture or killing of enemy forces – a clear reduction of the threat to forces in the field or, to put it in business terms, a concrete performance metric. For the intelligence teams, it was preferable to work on a mission that contributed to capturing or killing a high-value target, just as business leadership teams all over the world seek to show a tangible result, often at the expense of broader opportunities and increased understanding.

DATA FROM THE FRONT LINES

In Afghanistan during 2006-2007, people and groups in our environment were intrinsically linked in a way that joined all the colour categories together. So, a single individual could represent one or more colours at any time as shown in Figure 6.

FIGURE 6: AN EVER CHANGING FLUID PICTURE

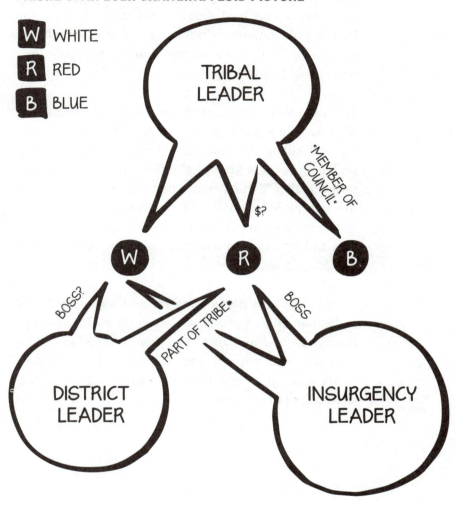

For example:

- A tribal leader (white) was also a member of the part-time district council (green/blue) and involved in part-time insurgency financing (red)
- A district leader (white) was also a member of a tribe that included insurgents (kind of red)
- The insurgency leader (red) was also a member of the tribe (white)

This web of conflicting loyalties manifested in many ways. We would hold district-level meetings with the local population, often sharing tea and food, only hours later to be facing some of the same people (part-time insurgents) in combat.

To add to this complexity, these identities and relationships were not static. It may seem obvious that isolating and killing the insurgency leader would solve the problem. But this kind of simplistic solution often led to unforeseen consequences that did not advance our mission. In fact, the death of the insurgent leader might have led a government official to seek out a more complex and perhaps more dangerous relationship, such as narcotics gangs.

We saw the host nation's military officers – supposed to be our allies (green) – constantly colluding with insurgents and allowing their family members to be involved with corrupt and illicit practices. Thus, it didn't seem at all like they were supporting what we were trying to achieve.

A FUSED PICTURE

A 2010 report from the Center for New American Security sums it up: "Intelligence in Afghanistan is enemy-centric, when it needs to be population-centric."

At the same time, another report, from the RAND Corporation, a non-profit US think tank, further explained: "Fusion is not only a function of analysis, but it is also a way of thinking about both the analytic problem and the analytic output. In this interpretation of fusion, everyone associated with the intelligence cycle would work from the proposition that collection feeds the development of a holistic analytic picture that reflects a best effort to describe both interdependent (between people and groups) and internal (within an individual or group) complexity."[19]

19 Rand Corporation. "Military intelligence fusion for complex operations," Occasional Papers, OP377 https://www.rand.org/pubs/occasional_papers/OP377.readonline.html

During our time in Afghanistan, we started to create fusion centres (stability operations with information centres) in which many of my former colleagues and friends operated. These were intended to build other intelligence capability and analysis, specifically from 'white' and 'green' areas – local businessmen, tribal leaders and government officials.

The image of a British marine sitting in a local meeting discussing the security of the area with a military officer, an army officer, a tribal leader, a businessman, an NGO worker and other coalition forces groups became commonplace.

So, at the front line of the organization in teams, the mindset shift was simple, to go:

FROM: What are the enemy doing?
TO: What is the situation?

The best place to find the truth is
to listen to your customers.
They'll tell you what's good about
your business and what's wrong.
And if you keep listening,
they'll give you a strategy.

Sir Terry Leahy
Former CEO, TESCO

Situational understanding was how teams won and lost. I recall that the only time I felt scared in the marines was not when bullets were flying around me, but when I started to lose situational understanding, as I knew this would lead to poorer decisions that could risk the lives of my fellow marines.

KEY CONSIDERATIONS FOR TEAMS

How can we increase our understanding?

- Are we focused too much on 'red'?
- What else should we be asking to build out situational awareness?
- What questions are coming from the front line?
- How can we identify all the critical external factors that could influence how a situation will develop?

_____

_____

_____

_____

_____

_____

PART TWO

TURNING DATA INTO UNDERSTANDING

For the value we've described to be realized, organizations will need to create leaders who are skilled in using the insights drawn from data in everything they do, and in building teams that operate with these insights through everyday interactions. Only by asking the right questions will teams be able to unlock the true value of data. There will be a shift from the Jack Welsh organization, where the executive is king, to the team-driven organization, in which teams are empowered to make decisions.

But teams will look different in the data age. Experience needs to be combined with new data skills, and successful teams will need to build the right capabilities to work with these new perspectives. Teams here will be messy, and comfortable with conflict, where advantage doesn't come from efficiency or a high-performing team focused on a goal, but rather one that is comfortable to challenge ideas and the 'plan'. The highest-paid person's opinion (HIPPOS) will no longer be held as gospel in a data-driven organization.

CHAPTER 5

MAINTAIN AN ENTHUSIASM TO SHARE

I have heard a story about a doctor who happened to sit next to an oncologist on a plane. They got to talking shop, and the oncologist mentioned using a drug with his cancer patients that was normally used for diabetes.

When the doctor expressed surprise, the oncologist explained that, during his 20 years of practice, he repeatedly saw patients with serious cancer conditions who recovered for no evident reason. After investigation, he realized that many of these patients were taking the diabetes drug. So, he began prescribing it for cancer conditions, with considerable success.

Now the doctor follows the oncologist's lead, prescribes the diabetes drug for cancer patients, and has been very happy with the results.

This is an example of how sharing insights leads to better performance.

Just as the Royal Marines learned to broaden thinking in the teams where information flowed from the front lines to the leadership, so businesses must build teams that are driven by sharing information and insights, breaking down silos in the process. What's needed is an organization-wide culture for the analysis of data, the extraction of insights, and the ability to turn those insights into action and share them.

When we talk about the deployment of data and analytics skills into organizations, we often refer to the quality of products and tools that are available. Little attention is paid to the quality of interaction between the domain and analytics expertise, quickly aligning to what's important and gaining a quick understanding of the business context. And, indeed, how the analysts and business leaders think in this new era of complexity.

As Mckinsey & Company puts it in a recent study, *Three Keys to Building a Data-Driven Strategy*: "Management must possess the muscle to transform the organization so that the data and models actually yield better decisions."

The challenge, for most businesses, is to develop a culture in which understanding permeates the organization. The concept of understanding, as a business culture, involves a kind of feedback loop: leaders set priorities for the business and give direction to the front lines. But the leaders' decisions are partially based on the experience of the front lines and what they are seeing in front of them, and the analysis of data based on the business challenges that those teams face.

Understanding cannot be based solely on experiences and views from senior leadership – it involves sharing insights across the organization, from the front lines to the centre and across the rest of the company. The chief data officer (CDO) plays a leading role in managing this process.

UNDERSTANDING AND THE CDO

INTRODUCTION

PART ONE

CHAPTER 1

CHAPTER 2

CHAPTER 3

CHAPTER 4

PART TWO

CHAPTER 5

CHAPTER 6

CHAPTER 7

PART THREE

CHAPTER 8

CHAPTER 9

CHAPTER 10

CONCLUSION

In the new organization created by the flow of data and insights, the CDO has an innovative role to play. There is no question that increasing numbers of CDO positions have been created at major corporations. According to Gartner, just five years ago only 12% of surveyed firms reported the appointment of a CDO. But, Gartner now predicts that 50% will have a CDO by the end of 2017.[20]

As Figure 7 shows on the next page, 48.3% of executives surveyed believe that the primary role of the CDO should be to drive innovation and establish a data-driven culture.[21]

20 Randy Bean, "How women are shaping the Big Data Revolution," Forbes, April 17, 2016 last accessed August 24, 2017 https://www.forbes.com/sites/

21 "Big Data Executive Survey 2017," last modified July 6, 2017 http://newvantage.com/wp-content/uploads/2017/01/Big-Data-Executive-Survey-2017-Executive-Summary.pdf

FIGURE 7: THE CHIEF DATA OFFICER'S ROLE IN CULTURE

THE FUTURE ROLE OF THE CHIEF DATA OFFICER.	
Drive innovation and a data-culture	48.3%
Manage data as an enterprise asset	41.4%
Ensure regulatory compliance	6.9%
Role is unnecessary	3.4%

Source: New Vantage Partners Big Data Executive Survey 2017

The CDO has two levels of responsibility: first, to manage the technical aspects of data collection and analysis, but, more importantly, to work closely with the CEO and other management to break down siloes and build a culture of sharing information and collaboration to the company. The CDO must champion sharing at every level, managing that feedback loop that needs to bring management and the front lines into the same mind-set using analytics to provide the shared insights.

Part of the CDO's role is to provide a coherent strategy for the organization. Most major companies are racing to get such strategies in place. Organizations need CDOs to take ownership of data, to manage and implement the processes around it.

Of course, most important is identifying the best customer-centric data for analysis, so that insight for improving the customer experience can be derived. This means that the CDO is closely connected with the front line, making certain that the best discussions around data are taking place. The CDO must then oversee the analysis meeting culture to ensure that teams are challenging groupthink and the bias and heuristics of leaders. And the CDO must take the insights derived from the front line and interpret them with top management. Here is where the CDO will either win or lose.

At discount broker Charles Schwab, for example, the CDO manages the cultural transition to data-driven collaboration. The CDO also has the minor roles managing data governance and data technology.[22]

"The most successful CDOs will be the ones who can distinguish themselves based on the organizational followership they develop. It goes beyond buzzwords of having a 'data-driven culture' and 'treating data as a corporate asset'. Success with big data rests with CDOs going beyond their own organization and evangelizing the opportunities possible with well-managed data. The CDO should help the organization look past reporting and rearview-mirror-use cases to see data as predictive, an enabler of new capabilities and value," Andrew Salesky, the CDO of Schwab, tells us.

The CDO works to create a community of workers who are continually identifying, evaluating and pursuing data-driven opportunities to advance the value a company provides to its *customers*. Part of the CDO's role is to make data more accessible, accelerating speed to insight and ensuring a robust, well-governed data environment. Finding the right individual to fill this role, obviously, is

22 Dataversity website, "Interview with Charles Schwab CEO Andrew Salesky," April 10, 2016, last accessed August 25, 2017 http://www. dataversity.net/ sep-1-cdo-webinar-chief-data-officer-interview/

not easy. The right individual has to be a technologist as well as a manager.

"A central theme of the chief data officer conferences is the requirement for nontraditional skills and experience when it comes to leadership of corporate data initiatives. The CDO is a change-management leadership role. The role requires a mix of business savvy, excellent communication and storytelling skills to engage the business, an ability to bridge technical and business domains, and collaboration skills, as data is a team sport," comments consultant Randy Bean, of NewVantage Partners.[23]

It has been said that data is storytelling, so good CDOs are good at communicating in business terms, understand how businesses use data, and can convince others of the business value that better data quality can bring. Communication and collaboration are essential. In the end, it comes down to culture change: most CDOs chair some kind of cross-functional committee of business executives, so they need to develop a strategy that delivers data value that breaks company silos.

"A significant piece of the role, which has not fully been recognized across the board in the industry, is the importance of change management. A lot of my job is spent listening to the business and its challenges with data, educating people on how their role in being stewards of data can lead to improved performance, helping develop solutions and breaking down silos, and demonstrating the business value of improving the data environment," explains Alison Sagraves, chief data officer at M&T Bank in Buffalo.

23 Randy Bean, "How women are shaping the Big Data Revolution," Forbes, April 17, 2016 last accessed August 24, 2017 https://www.forbes.com/sites/ciocentral/2017/04/26/how-women-are-shaping-the-big-data-revolution/#5d462854784e

CASE STUDY – CITY OF LOS ANGELES

A DATA-DRIVEN CULTURE FOR CITY ADMINISTRATION

Running a huge city like Los Angeles means asking lots of questions: "Can traffic be managed more efficiently?" "How can the city reduce the crime level?" "What elements would improve the quality of life in the city most rapidly?"

Since taking office in July 2013, Mayor Eric Garcetti has continually demonstrated his commitment to using data and analytics to solve issues in Los Angeles. He has committed his office to making Los Angeles, "the most open and transparent city in the US, by expanding the use of data and analytics to streamline service delivery and drive innovation in all operational processes."

In 2014, Garcetti appointed the city's first chief data officer to spearhead the adoption of a data-driven culture across his administration (the first one was Abhi Nemani, and he was succeeded last year by Lilian Corral).

"The culture change is easy to chart," Corral explained to me in an interview. "Usually city government has two levers, two methods, of taking action: there is a policy lever and a regulatory lever. We are trying and succeeding in changing that decision-making culture, so that working with data for solutions is tackled first, before policy-making and regulation.

"We've seen that rules and policy don't always work. Ask anyone, for example, about the city procurement system and they'll tell you it's broken down. The system is buried in a mire of rules and policies, layer after layer – you have to do paperwork at five different agencies just to bid on a contract. We're working to set up bypasses using technology so that the contractor can just get on a list, and not deal with five separate touchpoints."

Lilian pointed out to me that a mindset shift is necessary. "We will try to go to the data ahead of policy and regulation, so that city business workflow is determined in accord with citizen needs. This means a change into adopting design-type principles like those of the private sector – and this administration has championed this approach. It means using discovery-driven leadership, so that decisions are made after the data provides a clear view of the issues."

Making this kind of cultural change is not easy, she notes. "City government people say, 'I've been doing it this way for 15 years and now I have to change?'"

Since the beginning of the Garcetti administration, the city has created a whole series of initiatives, including Data LA, the Los Angeles Data Science Federation, and OpenData, among others. For cities, the impact of data has the potential to be no less transformational, and city halls around the country are grappling with how best to integrate this seemingly endless array of information into their decision-making processes.

The City has pulled together more than 1,100 data sets and layers, and it shares them all via the OpenData Platform. But, apart from making data available to citizens, the chief data officer is taking a slew of issues that citizens are concerned about and finding new ways to address them by going to the data.

Garcetti is committed to building a data-driven culture throughout the city administration, and he has implemented project after project based on data analytics. He sees data analytics as an essential part of the drive to make city services more efficient, and he has successfully used them for this purpose.

Garcetti's efforts were crowned last year by Los Angeles, earning the award for "number-one digital city in the country."

One of the key initiatives in breaking down data siloes and sharing information is the LA Geohub. This map-based platform uses geographic data to foster communication across city departments, spur innovation, and increase community engagement through storymaps and apps. The GeoHub has a city and public platform to maximize internal and external data sharing.

Using the Geohub, LA city departments can gather data for specific projects and find answers. For example, at the time of writing, Lilian Corral is working on a project involving parking management – at any given time, 30% of the cars on LA streets are searching for a place to park. Using the Geohub and other data sources, Lilian and her team can find not only basic numbers about how many cars versus spaces there are in the city, but also who is driving, at what times, what kind of cars and why people are driving at given times.

The city is taking insights from the data, and then working with Waze to share data back and forth to improve commuting and make it easier for people to find parking spots, Corral says. All this can help to 'crack the code' on parking, as she puts it.

A similar project is the list of 2015 registered foreclosure properties, which allows real estate developers to get to work on them faster, potentially changing the face of whole neighbourhoods by speeding development. Community groups also work with it to help keep struggling homeowners in their homes.

City officials from a number of departments have already made good use of the maps of criminal activity that the city now makes available. For example, it's been possible to analyse bicycle theft patterns using data from these maps, to show that there is a definite seasonal trend to the thefts, with many more taking place in summer than in winter – although not because there are fewer on the road in the colder season. It also becomes clear that most of the thefts take place in downtown or central Los Angeles.

And the Data Science Federation has built a model, in collaboration with local universities, that tracks and measures the social, cultural, and economic impacts of city-funded art projects.

Some projects take time. Corral's team has been working with the Department of Water and Power for more than eight months. "We wanted them to produce data at the zip-code level, so that we could track levels of consumption. They have been resisting that, citing various issues. So we said, 'What can we do that you need?' We've provided some insights that they have found helpful, and we're building a relationship of trust. We're getting more and better data from them now, and we hope to do much more. It's an iterative process."

LA has successfully used analysis of public works data to get the streets clean. This has been a priority for Garcetti, as residents had long complained that city streets were filthy and seemingly impossible to get the city to clean.

Last spring, the city launched CleanStat, a data collection and mapping system that allows officials to track illegal dumping, bulky items, litter and weeds, and establish cleanup priorities across 114 neighbourhoods.

Data collected by the mobile teams is compiled in a detailed map of the city, with each street segment rated as being clean, somewhat clean or not clean. The city publishes the map online so that anyone can get a color-coded view of how streets rank for cleanliness.

According to the *Los Angeles Times*, Garcetti's approach "shows signs of success. Since he took office, the overall cleanliness of city streets, curbs and alleys has improved,

while crews are responding faster to complaints of pot-
holes, illegal dumping and graffiti, a *Times* review of
public works data shows. It's all a notable change from
four years ago, when mounds of garbage, construction
debris and discarded couches clogged alleys in parts of
South LA, the central city and the east side."

During the first survey in early 2016, more than 370
miles of streets and alleys – mostly in south LA – were
so dirty they required immediate cleanup, the *LA Times*
says. By the end of last year, that figure had fallen to 91
miles, or about 1% of city blocks, the analysis found.

Los Angeles also boasts the most advanced traffic management system in the world. But lack of insights about
who was driving, when, under what conditions and for
what reason impeded the improvement of traffic management. A collaboration with Google's Waze, initiated
in 2015, has made it possible to bring these questions to
the data and get the requisite insights. City officials have
noted a gradual improvement in traffic management in
the city since the start of the program.

Another improvement for the city's streets, Street Wize
is an application developed on Geohub that keeps citizens informed about street conditions. Upkeep, persis-
tent roadwork and construction have negative effects
on drivers and residents. Street Wize helps alleviate this
by pulling data sets from planning departments to map
various capital and construction projects happening in
each neighbourhood. In addition, the tool improves
communication across city departments, so that they
can better coordinate project timelines.[24]

24 "Los Angeles
GeoHub,"
last modified
June 16, 2016
http://geohub.
lacity.org/

"All this has made it most exciting to be a leader in data analytics for the city in this administration," Corral concludes.

"We're seeing different streams of public and private data come together, and the results are changing our city – people are finding parking spaces faster, getting around faster and this is just the beginning."

BUILDING A CULTURE OF SHARING: UNCOVERING UNKNOWNS

A culture based on understanding is a combination of shared insights, shared experiences and shared directions. Under the aegis of the CDO, all staff, from top management to the front lines, should every day ask the question: "Where are we today? Where are we headed? How do we get there?" There should be a kind of continuing collaboration from all parts of the organization addressing these questions. Data and analytics provide most of the answers to these questions, and it is up to the leaders to make the entire team go to the data, ask the right questions, and translate the insights to all.

Breaking down siloes, in which specialized depart-ments keep insights from being shared, is a critical part of the process of building understanding. Siloes are contrary to this process, because they prevent the kind of collaborative discussion that is fundamental.

FINANCIAL REWARDS DON'T WORK HERE!

In his book *Drive*, Daniel Pink tells us that research in incentive experiments shows that when a team conducts a cognitive skill task, a larger financial reward leads to a poorer performance. It's the other way around to what we've been taught – i.e. higher performance, higher reward. Whereas Pink suggests that higher incentives lead to worse performance!

When a task gets more complicated
and requires some conceptual,
creative thinking …
financial motivators don't work.

Daniel Pink
Author, *Drive*

In preparation for writing this book, I interviewed a former member of the Royal Marines IX Group – Intelligence Exploitation. He shared with me the culture that he built on operations where he was responsible for a central intelligence and data unit that supported other units on the front line. In Afghanistan, he and his team checked every day what the intelligence officers in the combat teams needed to understand and confirmed plans and operational requirements. He described a subtle but important way of running these daily check-ins. Rather than informing them of the orders from the top and what they need to do, he started by asking, "What are you seeing?" In doing so, he gleaned highly valuable insights from these teams and, by building an environment of 'safe to share', he could swiftly break silos of best practice across the battlefield and push insights towards other teams where they were most needed.

Even though he had the most up-to-date technology available to him, he said it was through these human interactions where the real value and nuances were picked up. Technology doesn't do this – yet!

This is the mindset that must be changed when seeking to achieve a holistic approach to acquiring insights using date analytics.

For example, in an automotive parts organization based in the US, the employees were theoretically focused on the customer, but in reality they had other priorities. They were not really focused on the quality of the flow of data and insights from the front line to the strategic centre, which is of critical importance.

The challenge for this organization was to build a closer relationship with its customers, because automobile dealerships that were diversifying into providing additional services were stealing their market share by converting their customers' one time purchases into lifelong services.

To combat this, the culture of the organization had to change at every level. The organization had to reject its previous short-term financial focus and centralize its corporate culture and become a customer-centric organization.

For the company's leadership, this meant improving operational efficiency, which is a near-sighted focus, as this does not necessarily address customer concerns. So the management rolled out an ambitious plan, with the focus on standardizing processes and operational excellence at the individual store level, with sales training and delivering best practices.

But none of this really addressed the customer understanding required, nor did this centralized approach work when they wanted to build a data-driven culture on the front lines. The result was that performance suffered and leadership was replaced.

The further result of this near-sighted strategy was that the front line became all about efficiency, while analytics and insights remained at the top. You might call this ivory-tower analytics – since a small army of data analysts were based in corporate headquarters and provided analysis that never reached the people who needed it.

The lesson here is that teams need to feel that they can explore new ideas, express themselves and create a dialogue with management. They should have the confidence that they are supported by their management in such endeavours. This can, of course be a challenge to leaders who have to learn to do less in order to achieve more. In other words, these leaders act as facilitators to discussion and analysis, rather than the 'hands on the pumps' that they are perhaps more accustomed to.

ACHIEVING UNDERSTANDING

In a data-driven culture, it is understanding that enables teams to win. Understanding is defined as "the perception and interpretation of a particular situation in order to provide the context, insight and foresight required for effective decision-making."[25]

Context is a key word here. Understanding starts with experience, the knowledge obtained by long and perhaps bitter labour in a particular field. But situational awareness, that is, grasping the here and now, has to enlighten that experience. This is where data and analytics come in. Together, these factors inform the context (knowing why something has happened or is happening), and provide foresight (being able to identify and anticipate what may happen).

25 UK Ministry of Defence, "Understanding and Decision Making," Joint Doctrine Publication, December 1, 2010 https://www.gov.uk/government/publications/jdp-04-understanding

There are several components to understanding:

- Internal sources – these include our own formal education, historical precedent and practical experience
- External sources – including all purveyors of information, including media, colleagues, data and analysis

Together, these provide the basis of situational awareness and it is this that allows us to frame the analysis critical to the development of understanding (this will be discussed in more detail later). Such staged discussion and analysis must also account for opposing views and test thoroughly any resultant hypotheses. Analysis allows the development of comprehension (insight) and, combined with the application of judgment, leads to the development of foresight. Insight and foresight are the two key outcomes of understanding. This is a continuous process.

Essentially, organizations must establish teams in which the knowledge and experience of its employees, along with insights from data and observation, are all shared. These silos teams should be broken down and the company should focus its efforts on responsiveness to the customer. Relationship-building within teams (which we will discuss shortly) is an essential function of leadership in a data-driven culture. The goal is to coach these teams to form the basis for a better understanding.

UNDERSTANDING IS PERISHABLE

Things happen; things change. This is why understanding must be refreshed by new events and trends, time and time again.

So, organizations must regularly refer to data and refresh their knowledge of the customer and the context in which they are operating. This should be an iterative process that continues to fill the cup of understanding continuously!

CASE STUDY – UNILEVER

UNDERSTANDING ACROSS AN ENTERPRISE

At consumer goods giant Unilever, an initiative proposed by the firm's Consumer and Market Insights group (CMI) illustrates this process. CMI found that consumers are increasingly seeking brands and products that align with their cultural identity and lifestyle. The result is that local firms, particularly in emerging markets, are growing fast and strengthening their competitive positions.

A presentation to the operating board by CMI's head, Stan Sthanunathan, drew on this intelligence and on CMI's own review of what was happening. Sthanunathan walked the board members through an analysis of why local brands were growing, what threat this posed and how Unilever could compete. The presentation focused attention, catalysed the conversation about strategy and ultimately led to changes in both organization and mindsets.[26]

In the past, it would have been most unusual for a consumer insight function to take a leading role in the direction of an organization. But, as research from i2020[27] shows in a report, 67% of executives at over performing firms (those that outpaced competitors in revenue growth) said that their organization was skilled at linking disparate data sources, whereas only 34% of the executives at underperforming organizations made the same claim.

This is the kind of team organization that leads to understanding.

26 Frank van den Driest Stan Sthanunathan Keith Weed, Harvard Business Review, "Building an Insights Engine," September 2016, last accessed August 25, 2017 https://hbr.org/search?term=stan+sthanunathan

27 Ibid

UNDERSTANDING AT SCALE

Sharing individual understanding to achieve greater collective understanding can lead to significant benefits. A collaborative environment relies on information sharing. Without collaboration, attempts to develop a collective narrative are doomed to partial success or to failure.

This is why breaking down siloes is so important. In many organizations, the collection of specialized knowledge has been a path to success for managers or even whole departments. For example, often management became needed in organization teams, as they were usually the ones who understood certain areas of the business.

Siloes of this type have to be broken down by changing the culture of these managers and departments, so that they understand that collaboration will now be rewarded and that hoarding information will no longer be tolerated. As a data-driven culture takes hold of an organization, siloes should disappear naturally, as teams begin to exchange ideas and build solutions. It should become apparent to everyone that being part of this process is the path to success.

There has to be a feedback loop among managers, marketers, data scientists and sales. The front line is the place to gather data, which should be further informed with sales and marketing knowledge, and then insights should be drawn out of it. Management has to direct the data collection and analysis so that the key issues for the business are addressed. But the entire process is a shared one, in which management makes decisions, but the front line and the data experts weigh in on them.

This means disruption and change for most organizations. Making change of this magnitude is not easy. A survey for the World Economic Forum's report on digital transformation showed that only a quarter of the respondent organizations indicated a willingness to make change in order to compete.[28]

Just as the military had to make the effort to rethink, adapt and reorganize to take full advantage of the insights from data, so do organizations' businesses.

"Organizational adaptation is also needed to overcome fear and catalyse change. Management teams need to shift priorities from small-scale exercises to focusing on critical business areas and driving the use of analytics across the organization. And at times, jobs need to be

28 World Economic Forum, Digital Transformation, January 2016, last accessed August 25, 2017 http://reports.weforum.org/digital-transformation/

redesigned to embrace advancements in digitization and automation. An organization that quickly adopts new tools and adapts itself to capture their potential is more likely to achieve large-scale benefits from its data-analytics efforts."[29]

But so far, few organizations have made the necessary adaptations. Forrester Research reports that while 74% of firms say they want to be data-driven, only 29% say they are able to connect analytics to action.

According to Forrester, the organizations that do succeed are those that turn data into insights and actions by building systems of insight – *the business discipline and technology to harness insights and consistently turn data into action.* "Because, while most business insight efforts are one-way – data to insight to hoping for action – systems of insight close the loop between data and action with teams of people using the right processes and technology to continuously discover, test and implement insights in software and decisions. What's more, they create feedback loops that measure outcomes, and they provide the tools to experiment, learn, and optimize."[30]

29 David Court, McKinsey, "Getting impact from Big Data," McKinsey Quarterly, January 2015, last accessed August 24, 2017

30 Brian Hopkins, "Channel Partner Business Models in the Age of the Customer," March 16, 2016, last accessed August 25, 2017 http://blogs.forrester.com/brian_hopkins/16-03-09

EDGE-CENTRICITY

Every Marine and Soldier Is a Sensor

A report by the World Bank coins the apothegm 'edge-centricity" to define the new form of corporate organization mandated by analytics-focused companies.[31]

There is a need for organizations to increasingly look at streamlining decision-making without direct involvement by too many heads of functions. Enterprises need to pursue edge-centricity, where the focus of their core capability development is on the front line of their organizations, by pushing information decision-making authority away from the corporate headquarters to customer-facing points. Fashion shoe

31 World Economic Forum, Digital Transformation, January 2016, last accessed August 26, 2017 http://reports. weforum.org/digital-transformation/

producer Tommy Bahamas, for example, based on feedback from analytics, empowered front-line employees to make decisions and address concerns related to poor customer service.[32]

32 "Digital Transformation of Industries – World Economic Forum Report," last modified January 10, 2017 https://www.google.nl/ search?q=world+ economic+forum+ digital+transformation +January+2016&gws _rd=cr&ei=WoOeWef PAumB6ASQ8L2QAw

CASE STUDY – AMAZON

DIRECTION FROM THE FRONT LINE

Greg Linden is an Amazon executive today. But, when he was working as a relatively low-level developer in the early days of the company, he showed how innovation can come from the front line.[33]

Linden pioneered the idea of offering recommendations to shoppers based on what was in their basket at checkout.

"The idea of recommending items at checkout is nothing new. Grocery stores put candy and other impulse buys in the checkout lanes. Hardware stores put small tools and gadgets near the register. But here we had an opportunity to personalize impulse buys. It is as if the rack near the checkout lane peered into your grocery cart and

33 Gregg Linden, "Geeking with Gregg Linden," Gregg Linden blog, April 2, 2006, last accessed August 25, 2017 http://glinden. blogspot.nl/2006/ 04/early-amazon-recommendations.html

magically rearranged the candy based on what you are buying," Linden wrote.

But executives at the top didn't like the idea. They felt that nothing should distract consumers in the check-out process.

Although Linden was ordered to drop the idea, he built a test for it anyway and managed to get management to agree to run the test online.

"The results were clear. Not only did it win, but the feature won by such a wide margin that not having it live was costing Amazon a noticeable chunk of change. With new urgency, shopping cart recommendations launched," Linden wrote.

Linden points out that this is the culture that makes organizations innovative and, as a result, successful.

"I think building this culture is the key to innovation. Creativity must flow from everywhere. Whether you are a summer intern or the CTO, any good idea must be able to seek an objective test, preferably a test that exposes the idea to real customers."

In practice, edge-centricity means a dynamic inter-change of information among leaders, those on the front line and all the other operations of the organization. It is a kind of feedback loop, with information being shared by everyone in real time. As leaders manage the overall direction of the organization, they base their decisions on data and insights coming from both operations and the front line – while each of these can make certain kinds of decisions independently, as well.

Organizations are taking advantage of fundamental skill sets that already exist within them. Employees with the curiosity to ask the right questions and the ability to synthesize and leverage new data quickly are well suited to lead the big-data revolution within their organiza-tion. In reality, they are the revolution, but they must be supported with business processes that place value on gathering and using data, and that integrate data-driven decision-making.

Everyone in the organization should have their vision fixed on customer experience. The front line must relay back to the leaders how the customer experience value can be maximized. The leaders must make decisions about overall direction and resource allocation based on the understanding of the customer.

CASE STUDY – ROYAL BANK OF SCOTLAND

USING ANALYTICS TO DRIVE CUSTOMER SUCCESS

34 Jonathan Meyrick, "The Secret Life of Data – How Analytics is Transforming our Business," RBS Careers, April 18 2017, last accessed August 26, 2017 http://jobs.rbs.com/posts/the-secret-life-of-data-how-data-analytics-is-transforming-our-business

RBS is one of the largest banking and insurance groups in the UK and Europe, with about 13 billion pounds in annual revenue. From its headquarters in Edinburgh, the financial services group operates a wide variety of banking brands offering personal and business banking, private banking, insurance and corporate finance.

At RBS, purpose has been redefined in recent years. In the wake of the financial crisis, in which the bank received a 45-billion-pound bailout, RBS's mission changed. As head of data and analytics for commercial and private banking, Paul Holland explains.[34]

"We wanted to become:

- Stronger – Laying the foundation for sustainable and attractive returns
- Simpler – Making it easier for customers to do business with us
- Become number 1 for service, trust and advocacy by 2020."

The role of data analytics was to achieve these goals by creating a great customer experience and improve decision-making. To achieve these goals, they had to start out by asking the right questions. "When I started," Holland says, "we couldn't even determine how many customers we had – on a good day, you got 17 different answers to the question, and on a bad one."

One of the first changes made was to align questions and tasks. Questions from leadership to the analytics team had been fragmented, much of it low value. Now analytics filtered tasks and questions, ensured they were aligned with major objectives, and concentrated on adding value where it mattered.

CONSISTENT LANGUAGE, CLEAR QUESTIONS, GREAT TEAMS

So Holland began by clearing up the language that was being used across the company, which defined people, customers and operations. Then, data was inconsistent in format and access: it was spread out over the whole organization. Now it was brought to a single data warehouse and procedures for cleaning the data and analysis were centralized.

"But analytics is about teams," Holland continues. "We all have more or less the same technology; we all have more or less the same techniques. Having analysts who can add value like ours is clearly a significant advantage. But key to the process is having leaders and teams who understand both business objectives and know how to derive the right questions."

Leadership has also changed. RBS has put in team leaders who understand how to work with analytics, but who also can have a discussion with management about the broader goals of the company, he adds.

RESULTS

What are the results of this data-driven transformation? After nine years of losses, RBS has swung into the black with a net profit of 259 million pounds in the first quarter of 2017. Rating agency Moody's recently raised the bank's rating, saying that it was now securely making a profit across its banking operations.

Obviously, the bank's success at creating a data-driven culture is only one aspect of its move into the black. But analysts attribute the change of culture as a major factor in its turnaround.

To achieve this, RBS has created better, personalized connections with its customers based on its ability to make data and analytics a key factor. By analysing and under-standing its data better, its employees and customers are having more personalized and valuable conversations, be it online, face-to-face or over the phone, resulting in improved customer experience.

The bank has spent significant sums on training for employee transformation. Based on insights from data that allowed visibility into common themes of customer dissatisfaction, the bank identified areas for improvement and built better communication at those touchpoints. The front line has been provided with extensive coaching and interaction with the team leadership.

Part of this achievement involved getting staff on board. They have been trained to understand the value of a customer-centric perspective and have learned how to take issues that arise in day-to-day encounters with customers to the teams, so that data can provide better ways of resolving them. Engagement on the front lines has been crucial in RBS's ability to improve efficiency and build trust and loyalty among customers.

Recent studies by Forrester Research[35] show that companies that succeed in implementing this kind of organizational change are among the most successful. Your company's ability to create value for its customers will depend on how easily you can digitally augment your core capabilities and realign them to deliver the outcomes your customers really desire.

To do this, leaders have to empower people, giving them some effective ownership of their work. It's better for them to make mistakes, and have leaders show them how to change, than to enforce top-down direction that is uncertain and insufficient. "This requires a different kind of leadership from the top, too," explains David Kelley, founder of IDEO and the Stanford Design School.

"In the experiment-driven organization, leadership becomes less about making the big decisions on behalf of the organization. The role of a leader, whether CEO or head of a small team, shifts from providing the right answers to posing the right questions," Kelley says.[36] The age of asking the HIPPO (Highest-Paid Person in the Room) to determine strategy has ended.

35 Forrester Research, "Digital Transformation, B2B study," April 10, 2015, last accessed August 25, 2017 https://fr.slideshare.net/accenturebelux/digital-transformation-forrester-study-b2b-spotlight

36 Kermit Pattison, "David Kelley on designing curious employees," Fast Company, April 10, 2011, last accessed August 24, 2017 https://www.fastcompany.com/1746447/david-kelley-designing-curious-employees

CASE STUDY – APPLE GENIUS BAR

DIRECTION FROM THE FRONT LINE BUILDING CUSTOMER UNDERSTANDING

As the owner of Apple products, I always find the experience of going into an Apple Store and attending one of the coaching/help sessions most useful. The energy and helpfulness of the staff, combined with the overall effort in branding, and the look and feel of the Genius Bar, all contribute to this.

But it's Apple's ability to get closer to the customer – not only physically, but in terms of actually understanding how they're using Apple products in their daily lives – that is the clever or 'genius' bit. They don't do this through a centralized one-off survey or customer feedback, they do this on the front line. Every day.

The physical layout of the stores, and the skilful staff are but table stakes. While the staff engage in valid technical support, they are actively listening and interacting with their customers and then send these insights to a central bank of knowledge where they can be exploited and translated into the next wave of new products and innovations.

The employees are both knowledgeable of the products themselves and disciples of the organization's philosophy. Their training is disciplined with the APPLE dictum of "Approach customers with a personalized warm welcome, Probe to understand the problem, Present a solution, Listen for issues, and End with an invitation to return."[37]

37 "Product Strategies for the Tablet Market," last modified January 26, 2012 http://techreview magazine.blogspot. nl/2012/01/

THE POWER OF DISCOVERY

As the workforce becomes empowered at every level to use and provide data and insights, discovery becomes a key quality. Workers are no longer just accomplishing tasks, they are continually asking, "How can I make this better for the customer? Where can we make some changes?"

It's a new work culture, as the World Bank report explains. "One where employees are empowered to do more, independently, and where trial and error is encouraged. This works when these employees are inherently curious – and their curiosity can be satisfied by the ability to get answers to questions about how their digital services really perform."[38]

38 World Economic Forum Report, "Digital Transformation," January 2016, last accessed August 25, 2017 http://reports.weforum.org/digital-transformation/

Writes leadership consultant Aad Boot: "As a program manager supporting this strategic corporate transformation process, I witness daily how stimulating people to adopt a curious attitude makes a big difference and has a positive impact. Highly complex transformations like this one often bring people and teams into situations where there are no clear predefined answers and solutions, where people need to explore, need to get outside the ordinary routine, and learn new ways of looking at things to find new ways of working."[39]

It's critical, as this executive points out, for employees at every level of an organization to open up to change. When we successfully open up to change, we want to investigate it, to understand it, even if it puts us outside our comfort zone.

"With this attitude, you train yourself in finding patterns, connections, dependencies, mutual impact, which you didn't see at first. It will help you find new solutions in a changing business environment, rather than sticking to traditional 'right-or-wrong' reasoning. It will lead to better decisions. It will make you see the opportunities first and quite possibly give you the skills and relationships to take advantage of those opportunities," he says.

Discovery is a key quality for employees in organizations that seek to be adaptive and responsive in the data age. It's a trait that leaders can cultivate for themselves and communicate to others. It can be learned, and employees will acquire this skill if leaders make it clear that showing curiosity is rewarded. Research by George Lowenstein of Carnegie Mellon University[40] shows that the more we know, the more we want to know.

39 Aad Boot, "Why curiosity is a key business attitude for the future," Leadershipwatch, September 25, 2016, last accessed August 25, 2017 https://leadershipwatch-aadboot.com/2016/09/25/why-curiosity-is-a-key-business-attitude-for-the-future/

40 Loewenstein G, "The Psychology of Curiosity," Psychological Bulletin, vol. 116, issue 1 (1994) pp. 75-98 https://www.mendeley.com/research-papers/psychology-curiosity-review-reinterpretation-1/

Leaders should seek to employ individuals who demand to know as much as possible, who are ceaselessly curious about doing things better.

KEY CONSIDERATIONS FOR TEAMS

How can we turn data into action?

- Are we turning insights into action? Or are we gathering data to reinforce our thinking?
- Do we place the goal of increasing our understanding at the centre of everything that we do?
- How are we continually filling our cup of understanding?

CHAPTER 6
DISCOVERY-DRIVEN LEADERSHIP

*A CEO needs to focus more on
the platform that enables collaboration,
because employees already have all the data.*

Cristóbal Conde
Former President and CEO, SunGard

In the age of complexity and information overload, discovery-driven leaders operate in the top right-hand box of the quadrant shown in Figure 8 below.

FIGURE 8: DISCOVERY DRIVEN TEAMS

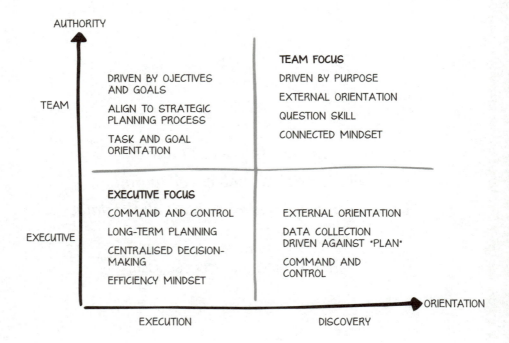

According to traditional definitions, leaders 'lead' and decide where the company goes next. Through this definition, it is clear to see that, traditionally, CEOs have a vision of how the business will succeed, and they give the orders to tell workers how to get there.

This image of leaders can be compared to that previously seen in the military, where, in the past, high-ranking officers made decisions and those below them simply carried out orders. Much of the traditional organizations in the West work in this way.

But, in contrast, the culture of the military has moved into the analytics age ahead of the business world, and now has a different dynamic. Having spoken to many military leaders during the research for this book, I realized that, despite the lack of technology, they certainly possess the right leadership capabilities required to get the most out of this resource. The military leader first goes to the data to gain situational awareness – current status and foresight for the next step – and then applies experience, know-how and judgment to determine the overall direction of the group.

The same process needs to take place in organizations. As the quadrant in Figure 8 shows, leaders move from execution to discovery, from a focus on delivering a financial plan to a focus on data-driven value guided by purpose. In today's highly uncertain, complex and fast-moving business environment, strategies should be about insight, rapid experimentation and evolutionary learning. The traditional leadership approach involving planning and execution are no longer adaptive enough to make a business succeed.

"Moving to a model of more data-driven decision-making is not as simple as buying a new IT system; it requires leadership to bring about lasting organizational change and usher in a new way of doing business," McKinsey & Company notes in a recent study, *The Age of Analytics: Competing in a Data-Driven World*. Effective leadership brings in a data-driven culture and then inculcates the process of leading with data.

At GE, for example, Ron Holsey, senior executive at GE Oil & Gas, took a hard look at his customers, as sales were declining. The upshot of data analysis showed that customers wanted solutions, not just technology. They no longer wanted to simply pay for technology products and instead demanded that hardware be linked to software and service solutions.

Holsey and his team determined that GE's industrial internet offers should become partnerships instead of mere sales and licensing agreements. They recognized the need for the organization to migrate away from a licensing-based pricing model to one based on a subscription model. Rather than charging a fixed price for a product, the subscription value is determined by whether a customer reaches a certain level of savings in operational costs. If that level is achieved, GE gets a cut. "If we improve, say, [a customer's] power consumption by X, we get $1; by Y, we get $1.50," explained Holsey.

Holsey and his team, after reaching an understanding of how their customers had changed, developed a new approach for customer relationships at GE, one in which GE and its customers must work together to realize those savings – they become co-creators of value. The example shows how the flow of data from the front line to the centre, combined with leadership experience and judgment, can lead to foresight and understanding – and successful business initiatives.

DATA FLOWS – PUSH AND PULL

But building a capability to increase flows of data from the front line to the centre is not easy. What we learned in Afghanistan was that leadership at all levels should understand that their direction is essential in leading and focusing the data effort. "Operations are command-led and intelligence-fed," became a slogan.

In a world of heightened complexity, success or failure will depend on the effectiveness of these data flows. We came across numerous examples while working in southern Afghanistan, where a tactical action could have a strategic effect, and the lines between the tactics and strategy with regard to data were often blurred.

Experience + Data = Understanding

Without an understanding of the situation at every level, it would be impossible for leaders to mitigate unintended second- and third-order effects. For example, in Afghanistan, we knew the importance of minimizing friendly force and civilian casualties and therefore limiting opportunities for insurgent propaganda to make use of them. Good intelligence – i.e., data and insights – was the foundation on which mission success was built. There was clear delineation between an area of operational responsibility and an area of intelligence.

The area of intelligence had to account for various influences that could affect the area of operational responsibility, such as tribal, ethnic, religious, economic or other inferences that transcend operational boundaries. Therefore, understanding what was happening within operational boundaries and sharing that understanding horizontally and vertically across organizations was critical. However, past organizational structures had always been built around a paradigm of "who else needs to know?"

This is particularly relevant for consumer goods companies, where brand insight in one location must be shared with other areas. Here is where silos are broken and real advantages can be found.

This mindset was built into us very early on in our careers and is a bedrock for the culture of the Royal Marines. During the early weeks of officer training, we were put through all sorts of inspections of our accommodation block, at all times of day and night. What was made clear was that at 2am the whole block would be inspected. In other words, if there was one weak link or crack, then everyone would suffer (and I literally mean suffer – running around in ice cold mud at 3 in the morning wasn't a rare occurrence). This meant that you were always looking out for your mates – your partners – to see if they needed any help or information. This mindset was in-built into all recruits and officers throughout the training process. It then becomes a natural instinct to always ask, "Who else needs to know this information?" during operations.

Information silos have nothing to do with technology. It's all about culture!

The maintenance of the picture from the front line, with all the complexities presented by tribal militia and criminal networks, is a dynamic process and intelligence staff had to routinely monitor and update its various strands throughout all stages of a counterinsurgency campaign.

The trick for us was not to fall back into traditional analysis, which focused on the enemy versus us. The enemy could be anywhere and everywhere, and could be almost anyone. Instead, we had to start with a question: "What was normal daily life like?" Against this picture, we could measure changes.

When it came to intelligence, there were many forms, and multiple sources were gathered from the front line. Soldiers and marines became the main collectors of information; they were the human sensors that fed insights to leaders for exploration when it came to intelligence.

Data from the Front Lines:

- **Human intelligence**, which could be collected by every soldier and marine, but had to be handled by more sophisticated intelligence personnel
- **Signals intelligence**, such as a conversation between people on a phone
- **Open source intelligence**, such as public expressions of attitude and public support from local media.

What was of critical importance in collecting these data points across the area of operation was that these were dynamic activities that were conducted continuously on the ground. Timely dissemination of insights from the front line to the leaders was of critical importance in maintaining a common picture, and data teams were continually asked for intelligence that leaders could share nationally.

TEAM DISCOVERY

Leaders should no longer simply be issuing orders; instead, leaders should be a part of 'feedback loops' that comes from both the front lines and from within the company. Leaders must be hands-off and allow those on the front line to build data and insights. At the same time, they need to have a focus on the bigger picture and understand the direction that the organization should be moving in. Having this mindset will help them ask the right questions to direct data collection and analysis.

So how do leaders position themselves for this new decision-making strategy? The stages discussed below provide a guide that can easily be applied to both leaders in business, as well as leaders in the military.

DOWN AND IN

Before combat, you start by making sure that everyone understands the plan. People need to know the 'why' behind what is being done, so that they can perform properly and innovate when they need to. Everyone has been sharing insights from intelligence, so that they know the background – many have helped to gather this same intelligence. We can say that the leader is looking **down** – at his employees – and **in to internal forces.**

Framing the 'what' and the 'why' for employees, but not telling them 'how', is of critical importance here. You provide the direction, then let them go. This is hands-off leadership and it can be very, very difficult. I have never mastered it myself; in fact, I'm not very good at it!

My junior leaders would tell you that I was far too 'hands on' with my team, not because I wanted to control them, but because I cared so much about them and felt responsible. This is a challenging paradox and one that I have never seen mastered, but it's a good practice to aspire to.

Hands-off leadership does work. A company commander from the UK Special Forces Support Group told me that when one of his platoons was in contact with the enemy, they dealt with it themselves, with highly decentralized decision-making and authority. Being hands-off allows the front line to make decisions that are timelier than a leader in the rear could make.

UP AND OUT

As I was driving past the explosion site in Kandahar and to the western edge where we would wait for the casualty evacuation team to meet up with us, I was telling myself:

- I need to inform other forces in the area about what has happened
- I need to inform my boss back in Helmand
- I might need to coordinate and link up with other forces

The pendulum had swung and, in this way, my thinking was in the **up-and-out** stage. This was about looking **up** to my leaders and **out** to external forces to make my decision.

The special forces company commander told me that during his time under enemy fire he reflected: "I have six helicopters turning up in two hours, how are we going to get out of here? Do I need to delay the pick up, what route should we take?"

He was starting to speak up the chain of command to align with other assets.

The art of leadership is recognizing when you need to intervene. To do this well, it is necessary to have an understanding of when your help is needed.

So, in my case, when the vehicle commanders told us that they were struggling, it was important to start moving teams around the battlefield so that others could support the one dealing with problems.

My advice to leaders is that when the panic alarm is going off, pull in your team and ask questions. Don't revert straight away to giving orders. Remember: *Innovation is about coming up with good questions, not good ideas.*

It's funny how, in the midst of chaos, you remember the smallest things. Once we had been hit by the IED, I remembered what my training officer had once told me: "Never underestimate the importance of the sound of your voice on the radio. Be calm. Take a moment. Act like a swan: your legs may be kicking like crazy and your heart pumping (mine was), but to everyone else around you, remain calm."

As I pressed the switch on my radio to inform the 60+ people under my command that day that all was OK, that casualties were being evacuated and a plan was in place, I remembered those words and did my best to sound calm and collected over the radio. I received feedback that my calm composure worked – even though I was kicking and panicking below the surface!

CASE STUDY – ROYAL DUTCH SHELL

ONE TEAM EFFORT!

For Royal Dutch Shell, adopting a data-driven culture was very challenging. Getting the different departments on board, breaking down siloes and building networked teams all proved to involve major changes to the way Shell personnel had worked in the past. There was resistance in changing the way teams operated, and moving away from statistic-based decision to data-based decisions.

As the head of the legal department for Royal Dutch Shell put it: "The best-planned process [of data-driven decision-making] in the world can be derailed by lack of stakeholder buy-in. Both execution and culture eat strategy for breakfast. Thus, as part of the panel review outreach initiative, senior legal leadership participated in a follow-the-sun communication workshop that focused on integrating legal units scattered around the globe and fostering a cohesive team ethos that cuts across time and distance."[41]

But Shell's successfully made the transition. As a study by Accenture and Microsoft in 2016 showed, 91% of oil industry executives felt that decision-making at their companies had been substantially improved by a data-driven approach.[42]

Royal Dutch Shell is one of the four largest energy producers in the world. Operating in more than 70 countries, Shell employs 92,000 people, produces 3.7 million barrels of oil per day from its 22 refineries around the world, and 57.1 million tonnes of liquid natural gas per year.

In its Upstream division, Shell focuses on the exploration for new liquids and natural gas reserves and on developing major new projects where technology and know-how add value for resource holders. In its Downstream division, the company focuses on turning crude oil into a range of refined products, which are moved and marketed around the world for domestic, industrial and transport use. In addition, they produce and sell petrochemicals for industrial use worldwide. Shell's oil sands mining activities in North America are also part of the Downstream organization.

The search for new hydrocarbon deposits demands a huge amount of materials, manpower, logistics and costs. Drilling an oil well can cost in the hundreds of millions of dollars.

For some time now, Shell has been developing the idea of the 'data-driven oilfield' in an attempt to bring

41 Vincent Cordo and Case Flaherty, "People as a bridge from data to info," April 25, 2016, last accessed August 25, 2017 http://www.accdocket.com/articles/people-as-a-bridge-from-data-to-info.cfm

42 "Accenture Oil and Gas Survey 2016," last modified; not available https://www.accenture.com/us-en/insight-2016-upstream-oil-gas-digital-trends-survey

down the cost of drilling for oil. But Shell is also using big data to redefine its approach to consumer products and in improving the efficiency of its transport and other operations.

"Oil and gas industry leaders continue to look to digital technologies as a way to address some of the key challenges the industry faces today in this lower crude oil price cycle," said Rich Holsman, global head of digital in Accenture's energy industry group. "Making the most of big data, the Internet of Things and automation are indeed the next big opportunities for energy and oilfield services companies, and many are already starting work in these areas."

They are increasing investments in enabling people and assets, with a growing emphasis on developing data supply chains to support analytics projects that can improve efficiencies, manage cost and provide a competitive edge.

Shell focuses their digital investments on areas where they see tangible business value. In the short term, given the low oil prices, oil and gas companies are focusing these investments on areas that deliver more immediate benefits in cost reduction. This includes lower operations costs through increased worker productivity with mobility, lower infrastructure costs through the use of cloud technology and better asset management through analytics. Over the next three to five years, investments are expected to shift to focus on areas that deliver the greatest long-term value, such as more comprehensive predictive operations management capabilities.

As a result, they are engaged in building the right skills in teams. Shell has implemented a mandatory training programme for data-driven communications, according to Sherine Yap, global head of CRM at the company. Yap explains that business-wide initiatives help create an understanding of information and insight. The training is, above all, about, 'understanding', so sharing insights from data and reports acquired at the front lines are used to meet customer demands.[43]

She says communication is crucial and that language barriers often persist. "Marketing and data teams should move closer together and explain in simple terms the likely outcomes of the insights being creating," says Yap. "Working in that way has allowed me to take information, package it up and share it with the wider teams across the business."

Shell makes use of insights from data for each type of production it is involved in. In oil well production, companies used to have to depend on a few statistics to choose a drilling site. Today Shell monitors the seismic waves below the surface of the Earth and generates millions of observations that lead to a decision on whether to drill or not. By analysing this data in the same way that one might analyse the actions of consumers, Shell can identify significant patterns to help make these decisions.

Throughout its other operations, like supply-chain management or transport, Shell can use data analytics at every stage of the processes to increase efficiency. Says Shell Downstream CIO Craig Walker: "As CIO, you think of all the businesses and look at the potential disruptions there – because you can bet your bottom dollar I know where the money's made on that value chain."[44] Walker adds that the company is exploiting magnificent opportunities at every level of the organization thanks to its data-driven culture.

43 Derek du Preez, "How Shell has bridged the gap between marketing and data," Marketing Week, March 24, 2017 last accessed August 24, 2017 https://www.marketingweek.com/2017/05/24/shells-brand-marketer-data-specialist/

44 Derek du Preez, "Shell Downstream CIO: We should be scared," Diginomica, May 23, 2017, last accessed August 25, 2017 http://diginomica.com/2017/05/23/shell-downstream-cio-scared/

On the consumer front, Kenyata Martin, head of marketing strategy, Shell Oil Products, North America, says that actionable integration of data promotes consumer engagement. Martin gave the example of Shell's use of customer feedback as a way to not only listen to and connect with their customers, but also to use that data as input for making product changes.

ACHIEVING MESSY TEAMS

Achieving a communication model for discussion of insights and for implementing the solutions that emerge from them has been a major achievement at Shell. Yap points out that this involved overcoming barriers to information-sharing and language barriers.

In an organization of Shell's size, achieving communication across cultures, departments and geographic boundaries is no small matter. By maintaining a clear and uniform language for sharing insights, Shell has been able to create and maintain a connected culture.

ON THE ROOF

Some leaders can't see the bigger picture. They don't have time, because headquarters is shooting at them with demands for the day-to-day. Or they just don't have the capacity to look over the horizon. But the most effective way leaders can direct their organizations is by seeing the entire perspective and making the decisions necessary when danger looms.

The special forces company commander told me: "As a leader, I often found myself implementing control measures, like telling a team not to move any farther south than a specific point on the map. The team members didn't like that, because they wanted to keep fighting. But as the leader, I had seen the bigger picture and I was observing and making decisions from the roof. Also, my experience told me that if the teams proceeded, the team could overexploit itself and create a space of vulnerability, which the enemy could take advantage of."

Putting yourself on the roof is a critical position for leadership today. It improves your view, but sometimes exposes you to enemy fire (internal and external); it's crucial to get the balance right and identify if the benefits outweigh the costs or risks. On the battlefield, this is an issue with physical consequences, but it is just as real an issue in the office. In organizations, leaders want to get the perspective they need, while remaining close to the front lines.

Leaders need to position themselves close enough to the action to know what's going on and have situational awareness and practice agility. The military has moved away from preparing a plan and working it to death to trying to accept and foster flexibility and initiative.

Agile leadership in business must do the same. The process starts with asking the following questions:

- Where are we now?
- What do our customers want now (not last week, not next year)?
- What will the competition do?
- What do we think are their key capabilities?

Data can provide the answers to these questions.

The organization must have the agility and flexibility to adapt each time to what is really happening. They must not become wedded to plans that have been created months prior and are slowly cascading into the organization.

Agile leadership should seamlessly adjust to intervening and directing from a hands-off mode. The gauge of a great leader is one who can make this adjustment exactly as needed, and as much as needed. Protecting employees too much results in insulating them and yourself from what's really happening. By directing employees too much, you won't be able to listen to the feedback and insights that only they can contribute.

So, agility and the capacity to adjust quickly are key for leaders. Do you intervene or not? Is the team running smoothly by itself for now, so that you can look ahead to next month, or next year?

Leaders need to be ambidextrous in this sense.

Leadership is a team sport rather than an individual sport. You put together this diverse team and install in them an 'it's all up to us' mindset. Then you're really a coach and you're just making course corrections.

KEY CONSIDERATIONS FOR TEAMS

How can we build a discovery driven team?

- Are we coming up with the right questions about our customers? Or are we fixed on finding the right answers?
- How are we committing to improving our thinking skills?
- Are we effectively harnessing the experience of this team?
- Are we on the roof or in the weeds?

CHAPTER 7

MILLENNIALS AND A BIG-DATA CULTURE

*Any complex task is best approached by
flattening hierarchies. It gets everybody
feeling like they're in the inner circle,
so that they develop a sense of ownership.*

General Stanley McChrystal
Author, *Team of Teams*

"By all accounts, millennials are unlike preceding generations. They view the world differently and have redefined the meaning of success, personally and professionally. In some cases, this has led to misunderstanding among the different generations coexisting in today's workplace. Increasingly, however, business leaders are realizing this generation's unique competencies and perspective, and employers are looking for ways to harness their strengths,"[45] UNC Kenan-Flagler Business School notes in a recent report. We will see below that messy teams will win in a data-driven company that fosters collaboration and discussion among leaders, the front lines, and the other parts of the company.

Millennials will make up approximately half the workforce by 2020 and so will make up a large part of the teams in most organizations. It will be a leader's responsibility to attract millennials to the company's teams and to keep them there.

But the problem with millennials is that they lack engagement at work. A Gallup study completed in 2015 showed that only 29% of millennials are engaged at work, while **16% are actively disengaged**. What does that say about the remaining 55%? When people aren't engaged, they demonstrate this by quickly leaving for another company.[46]

45 Brack, Jessica, and Kip Kelly. "Maximizing Millennials in the Workplace." Kenan Flagler Business School. 2012. http://www.kenan-flagler.unc.edu/executive-development/custom-programs/~/media/DF1C11C056874DDA8097271A1ED48662.ashx.

46 "McKinsey Global Institute The age of analytics: Competing in a data-driven world," December 2016 http://www.mckinsey.com/business-functions/mckinsey-analytics/our-insights/the-age-of-analytics-competing-in-a-data-driven-world

FOSTER A COLLABORATIVE ENVIRONMENT EVERY DAY

Millennials can thrive in a data-driven culture, because they love collaboration. This isn't about coffee and beanbag chairs, this is about the way that we interact with each other in meetings. Millennials routinely rank corporate culture as a major factor in how well they feel engaged. They want to work across teams and departments and don't respect corporate planning cycles or business unit silos (brilliant!). Organizations should cultivate and encourage these collaboration and cross-functional development opportunities, not only to get the most out the future workforce, but to build an effective data culture.[47]

47 Frank van den Driest Stan Sthanunathan Keith Weed "Building an Insights Engine," Harvard Business Review, September 2016 https://hbr.org/2016/09/building-an-insights-engine

215

Fostered collaboration is the number-one attribute for millennials in the workplace, according to a Microsoft study.[48]

We have all read that millennials are unsocial, that they sit by their screens and pay no attention to people. Whether this is true or not, leaders need to get them away from their computer and tablet screens and into challenging debates within teams and engage with data through purpose.

And, contrary to the belief that millennials are digitally isolated, the research above shows that the majority of respondents said "good team collaboration" was the most valuable attribute in their ideal workplace. The data showed that more than half these individuals have jobs that require frequent work on teams. Sixty-five per cent preferred face-to-face meetings with their managers and 51% preferred to have in-person meetings when collaborating with others on projects.

In the information age, the relationship between manager and employee is going to grow in importance. It is a vital link in performance management. The quality of communication between manager and employee must be kept high for that relationship to succeed.

Millennials don't relate to annual plans or planning processes and certainly don't respond to flashing red, amber or green lights on a dashboard that relate to their boss's metrics.

Millennial employees are found to be more engaged than non-millennials when their leaders communicate frequently and consistently and provide good feedback. It's all about feedback, making sure that they're on track, that everyone is on the same page, and staging an

48 Cindy Bates, "Survey reveals four secrets for attracting and retaining Millenial talent," Microsoft Business Blog, February 12, 2016, last accessed August 24, 2017, https://blogs.business.microsoft.com/en-us/2016/02/12/4761/

interactive discussion and debate over issuing orders. They want to feel that they are contributing to the development of the organization by adding to its understanding, innovation and important discussions.

One weakness of millennials is the inability to prioritize effectively, whereas other generations experience this much less so. Therefore, leaders should be aware and intervene to overcome this obstacle. Nearly 7 in 10 millennials strongly agree that guidance from leaders in establishing priorities keep them engaged, according to the Microsoft-Accenture report cited here.

Focus them on the important bits and let them go!

Millennials also place high importance on the purpose of the organization that they work for. As discussed earlier, this presents an exciting opportunity for organizations and their new workforce as they start on a path of data discovery using purpose as a handrail.

---

*No action, activity, or process is more central
to a healthy organization than the meeting …
this is where values are established,
discussed and lived …*

Patrick Lencioni
Author, *The Advantage*

Even with the best technology and data talent available, establishing an effective data meeting culture is crucial for success. For the data analysts, it's about understanding the mission and all the analysis that has led up to it. For the front-line commanders, it's about getting to the most meaningful insights to inform mission-critical decision-making. Both teams must ask questions in this iterative discussion to gather as much context as possible and build situational understanding. When trust is built and the teams come together with a common goal, it is hard to tell the difference between the two parties.

The results of getting data meetings right:

- Broaden team understanding of future clients, customers, market needs and pains
- Identify bias, groupthink and flawed assumptions
- Avoid the tendency to jump to the wrong conclusion because of the loudest voice
- Connect relevant data to the most important business challenges and priorities

Success in a data meeting comes down to three attributes:

- **Diversity of the team** – invite data scientists and business leaders from across the organization. Diversity of thought is your competitive advantage here
- **Application of the right tools** – Keep it simple. Data science isn't scary, but let the experts handle the complicated stuff
- **Support from leadership** – Leaders need to stage the right discussion and come prepared to listen and be challenged

Data meetings are not like regular check-ins or planning conversations; they should feel different from the start. Teams should be scrutinizing and challenging thoughts, ideas and assumptions to consider the perspectives of data talent and external players. The best business leaders open themselves up to be challenged not only by their own teams, but also by analysts from outside the core team who are providing insights. Senior military commanders will even stage an 'alternative thinking team' tasked to deliberately challenge current thinking.

RED FLAGS FOR A MEETING CULTURE

We are all subject to bias, emotion and groupthink. If we are gathering data to confirm something, we may experience confirmation bias. Or having worked so hard on a project, we may let our emotions control conversations, which immediately affects the potential of data.

Recent events such as Brexit and the Chilcott Enquiry have shown how groupthink can be so dangerous and how decisions made by leaders, even at the most strategic level, can be affected by groupthink. Teams need to feel safe in order to effectively challenge and debate issues that have surfaced through looking at data – the days of following the highest paid person's opinion (HiP-PO) are gone in data meetings.

Here are some guidelines that you can apply to your data team meetings immediately to drive an effective meeting culture:

1. Challenge assumptions
2. Identify flawed logic or analysis
3. Assess the quality of the data
4. Identify alternative options and **adapt** your plans
5. Test a plan or perspective through the eyes of someone outside your immediate team

COMFORT AND RESPONSIBILITY

Comfort in the workplace is also extremely important to millennials, as research indicates. Millennials want a work environment that is comfortable and that inspires them to contribute without fear of being criticized. This makes them perfect for messy teams, in which they can speak out, challenge and exchange ideas freely with both leaders and colleagues.

What's more, contrary to the irresponsible label millennials are stereotyped with, they actually value accountability in the workplace. On the contrary, millennials want to be held to account, and they want credit for good work – this is very important to them.

It's true that older employees also demand clear-cut accountability, to know what's expected of them in the workplace. "The generations preceding the millennials are sort of like cowboys, a rugged, individualistic lot. In general, these baby boomers and Gen Xers believe in a command-and-control management approach, value working individually, view managers as experts and look to their employers for career planning. They like clear boundaries and have a generally inward-looking perspective as compared with millennials," Marc De Swaan Arons notes in the Kantar report.[49]

Millennials reject the command-and-control paradigm. They have grown up with technology and are accustomed to researching ideas with multiple sources, using the different tabs on the browser. They are accustomed to working on their own with the help of coaches and mentors, and this is part of management's role in keeping them engaged.

Participation in messy teams offers millennials the kinds of opportunities that they look for. They can share ideas, but they can also get credit when they come up with good ones themselves. They can work directly with leaders, as leaders integrate into the teams, but they don't have bosses telling them what to do. They share in the decision-making process and understand the direction in which the company is going and feel part of it. When they don't, they leave.

Having grown up with easy access to advanced technology and the internet, millennials are tech-savvy multi-taskers because that is all they have ever known. This means that the process of seeking insights from data before action suits them well. The term *multi-int* (multiple sources of intelligence), used in the military intelligence

49 Marc de Swaan Arons, "Building an Insights Engine," Kantar US Insights, November 18, 2016, last accessed August 25, 2017 http://us.kantar.com/business/brands/2016/building-an-insights-engine/

field, matches the way millennials see the world and act on it, as well. They expect to keep discovering and learning, and they use any number of sources to feed their creativity and curiosity.

So, it is natural that they should seek a different relationship with management than their predecessors. They don't view managers as content experts as previous generations did. Rather, millennials know where to find multiple versions of the information themselves and view managers more as coaches and mentors. They see life in more circular, optimistic terms.

Where millennials act as managers themselves, they will personalize their management techniques. They do not take on the role of a traditional boss, but instead embrace their own unique working style, helping shape and mould a more positive corporate culture by encouraging people to be themselves and speak their minds. Millennials are more likely to rely on professionalism when working with those from previous generations, similar to if those from older generations were contractors called in for their expertise. This works well sometimes, but not in all cases.

This is great news for data, because managers who fear to challenge their boss and the team's thinking and groupthink, bias and heuristics limit the value of big data. If the research is accurate, my view is that millennials are going to carve the way forward in teams using data.

As managers, millennials expect teams to have the same abilities with social media and technology that they have grown up with. But they also like to stand out in a group, expressing their own personalities and allowing others to express theirs. They welcome discussion and debate, but may also wish to dominate it. What they are unlikely to accept is groupthink, and this again is a positive characteristic for teams in a data-driven corporate culture.

Millennials will soon make up an increasing part of the workforce, and as organizations compete to acquire and retain the best talent, transformation into a data-driven culture will come through increasing pressure from within. Millennials will demand that management makes a substantial investment in data initiatives and they will help in breaking down siloes and democratize access to information. In a genuine and authentic way, millennials will lead the way in building a culture that is passionate about data-driven decision-making.

This is why managing millennials productively will provide a strong competitive advantage as companies seek to become more data-driven. For organizations, it's time to change. Not only to reap the benefits of institutionalizing a data-centric culture across departments, but also to engage and retain the next generation of millennial talent. These individuals thrive in data-rich environments, and data can be used to fuel their professional growth, power cross-departmental dialogue and drive key decisions.

KEY CONSIDERATIONS FOR TEAMS

How can we build teams for the future?

- Are we listening to different perspectives?
- Are we letting ourselves be challenged?
- How can we challenge our HiPPOs in a safe way?
- How can we nurture new talent through our daily interactions?

PART THREE
SKILLS AND LANGUAGE

Teams in this organization won't be passive audiences watching PowerPoint slides. They will need a new set of skills.

Understanding will become the key quality for teams. The ability to frame questions that will shape enterprise objectives must come from every part of the company. Connecting with teams empowered to develop ideas and take action is critical.

Language will be of critical importance here, as the quality of interaction between domain and analytics expertise in teams will separate the winners from the losers. Clarity around what is trying to be achieved from the business perspective and the analytical methods that need to be applied will be of critical importance. Organizations that industrialize a simple and common language to close this gap will be able to operate at a faster pace – the source of competitive advantage.

Finally, it's an organizations' ability to connect these teams with each other that will really separate them from the pack. Everything starts with trust, and leaders' and teams' ability to translate insights vertically and horizontally throughout the organization will start to build an insights-driven community and a data ecosystem. The organizational output here will be unlocking the power of all the teams, and big data aligned to what's important. Purpose.

CHAPTER 8
BUILDING "MESSY TEAMS"

*It's not the biggest, the brightest
or the best that will survive,
but those who adapt the quickest.*

Charles Darwin

We have spoken about how leadership has started to change in the data age: a shift from the executive to the team and from an execution to discovery-driven orientation. Now, as we talk about how teams are changing, I introduce the concept of 'messy teams'.

Making decisions in a world of information abundance, where we have moved from not having enough information to an explosion of data, is not easy. It requires a change in the usual high-performing team paradigm from a linear path of execution to an iterative path of discovery;

From:

- ✓ Define the objective
- ✓ Collect perceived relevant Information
- ✓ Generate options
- ✓ Make the decision
- ✓ Implementation and evaluation

Here, the traditional use of data is used to augment a pre-ordained plan in a linear way, getting from A to B as shown in Figure 9.

FIGURE 9: TRADITIONAL TEAM LENS IN STABLE ENVIRONMENTS

To:

- ✓ Align to what's important
- ✓ Ask a forward-thinking question of the data
- ✓ Conduct a team analysis
- ✓ Make a data-driven decision
- ✓ Translate to those who need to know

Here, data feeds the adaptive capability in teams through rapid iteration as shown in Figure 10 on the next page.

INTRODUCTION
PART ONE
CHAPTER 1
CHAPTER 2
CHAPTER 3
CHAPTER 4
PART TWO
CHAPTER 5
CHAPTER 6
CHAPTER 7
PART THREE
CHAPTER 8
CHAPTER 9
CHAPTER 10
CONCLUSION

FIGURE 10: ADAPT CYCLE

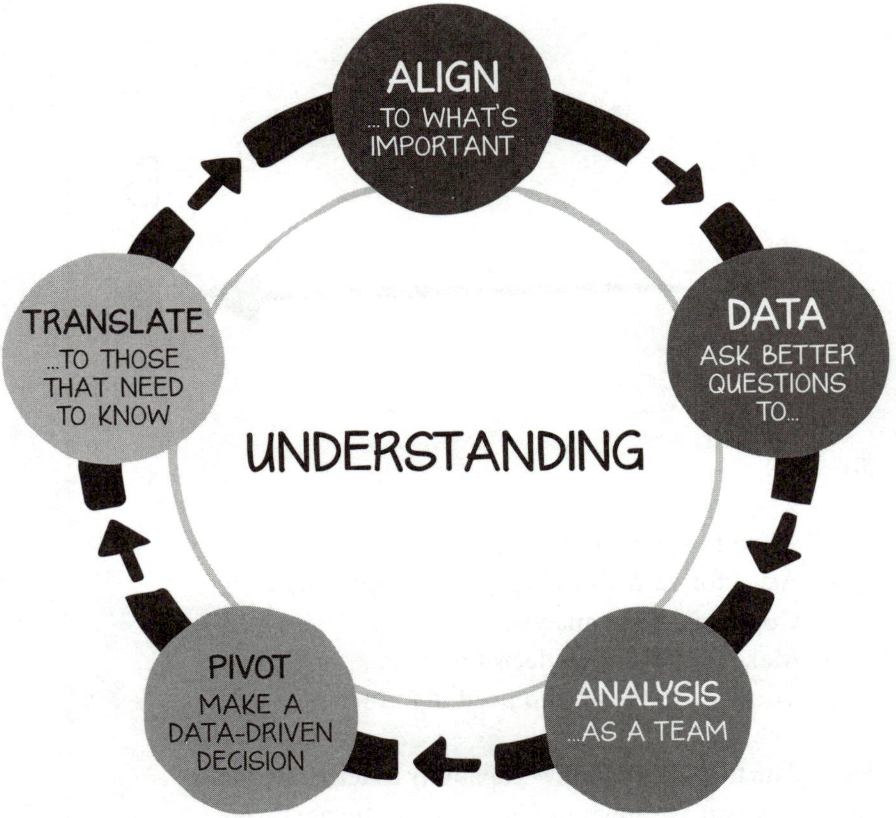

ADAPT Cycle: Copyright © Connectworxs 2017

While each step of this cycle may be simple and intuitive to follow, at each one there is a distinct mindset shift in leaders and the team as shown in Figure 11.

FIGURE 11: TEAM MIND-SET SHIFT

FROM	TO
Team execution	Team discovery
Data report requests	A data questioning skill
Executive	Team
Gut decisions	Data decisions
Silo	Network

I don't need to know exactly what I'm looking for, as I 'know' all data is available.

Now that the focus on the customer has become critical, companies must transition from a top-down leadership style of giving goals and objectives, to sharing data and insights from the front lines across all teams, achieving understanding so that the right decisions can be made. However, this does not increase your team's ability to know what is the right data required to make the right decision. The volume of information and data – and indeed the requirement to integrate numerous sources – can often result in information overload and decision paralysis.

This is not just about working with new technology. Over reliance on technology leads to failure. Human factors are what make the difference in the data-driven business world of today.

Messy teams are created through rebalancing team members and the use of big data analytics. It also involves changing the way in which we interact with each other every day when working in teams. Messy teams provide the means for good decision-making by restructuring how decisions are made from the traditional top down paradigm. The human factor, in my experience, and cultural orientation, drive decision-making, whether in business or in the military. As we strive to become data-driven organizations, these are the challenges we must address. This looks like Figure 12.

FIGURE 12: MESSY TEAMS

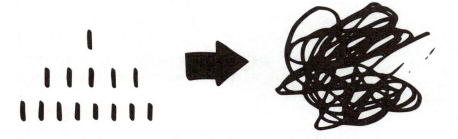

In contrast to the manufacturing age, we now operate in a business world of heightened complexity, where commercial success will be won at the front line under the glare of highly demanding customers. If teams are going to be successful, they need to be comfortable operating in such complexities and face challenges with varying degrees of problems.

This is like the challenges that the armed forces have been faced with over the past decade. We had to be prepared to fight, keep the peace and protect the population, while at the same time managing interactions and tensions among competing imperatives and activities. I recall listening to one of my colleagues talk about leading his team of soldiers in Basra, where they were fighting a war one day, and handing out bottles of water to school children the next – on the same streets.

In the face of complexity and information abundance, teams require a new set of skills so that a team's collective effort produces the right questions to ask. This teamwork should replace the paradigm of top-down leadership imposing direction through goal setting. The leaders should be integrated into the team effort, but also able to use the insights from the team in combination with overall direction.

The thinking process in the team environment needs to be re-explored, with an understanding of how bias and heuristics can influence teams in different ways. It's also important to understand the critical distinction between intuitive and analytical thinking, and the impact of this as we attempt to close the gap between domain expertise and analytics talent in teams.

It is through the rituals and ways of thinking and working that messy teams will be successful. Balancing thinking between experience, know-how and data is one part and establishing the right group dynamics is another; building the requisite attributes and skills and instilling trust is yet another necessary aspect.

The nature of business today means that teams need to make decisions quickly and look for the factors that influence thinking and the ability to apply multiple perspectives.

BUILDING MESSY TEAMS

In this environment, teams need to have a more innovative response to complexity. Teams faced with challenges such as mass industry disruption from start-ups, economic instability or political uncertainty must leverage diversity of thinking to ask the right questions.

My personal experience from business school and the corporate world is that leadership and development departments and leadership training are dominated by programs such as *effective teamwork* and *high-performing teams*. I believe that this theory has been born of a more stable environment and is not suitable for the complexity that we now face. Effective teamwork and high-performing teams are, of course, still relevant, but these are table stakes and are not where teams will find a competitive advantage in the information age. Traditional thinking in teams will have to pivot from one way of thinking and act swiftly.

There will, of course, always be the time to just get on with it and execute!

Teams need to build a set of practices that I characterize as rituals, checklists and challenging techniques that will help them develop valid data-driven decision-making. These resources should not be available only to the top management team, but rather to teams throughout the organization, especially those closer to the front line.

Messy teams are committed to establishing the following habits and behaviours through everyday interactions:

- Openness and willingness to change minds by not 'falling in love with the plan'
- Feel comfortable working with uncertainty
- Use frameworks and checklists to explore different perspectives from both domain and analytics expertise
- Challenge assumptions through every decision
- Never stop at the first good idea
- Use competing hypotheses rather than seeking a data report to support a preferred theory

The winning skill of teams moving on to the information age will be the ability to balance the thinking skills for any particular scenario. They will be able to avoid an over-reliance on analytical thinking and employ the right techniques to trigger lateral thinking to gain new insights and situational awareness. Teams need to attract other members from the organization with a particular thinking style as an advantage point to their discussions and give them a clear remit to challenge, challenge, challenge. This alternative thinking style will be of critical importance when dealing with large, complex situations.

Don't overthink this and you certainly don't need external experts to help you here. Go and find this talent in the corners of your office – it exists. They know your business better than anyone. People with different perspectives of the challenges in your organization are everywhere – likely in the bank of desks opposite from you right now.

The biggest risk and opportunity for big data lies in the team. Get the team rituals right and teams will be in a strong position to embrace analytical thought. Teams also need to be aware of and consciously manage the wrong group dynamics for the data age. With these techniques, teams should try to bridge the divide between analytical and domain expertise as shown in Figure 13.

FIGURE 13: BRIDGING THE GAP

THE EXPERIENCED DOMAIN EXPERT	THE HIGHLY SKILLED ANALYTICAL EXPERT
Operates under consistent time pressure, reacting to other events from the wider team	Useful when accuracy and evidence are needed and information is available
Vulnerable to bias and heuristics	Less influenced by emotion
May use valuable situational information unconsciously built over time – 'grey hair' experience	May fall victim to silo thinking
Comfortable with unstructured problems and business complexity; familiar with politics	Some tools and techniques that have been developed in the tradition of objectivity; less familiar with politics
Large capacity for parallel thinking	Tendency towards linear thinking

Psychology grossly divides thinking into two categories: intuition and analysis. There is that which we know from analysis and examination, and that which we know without thinking.

We don't need a rigorous definition of this dichotomy. I don't think it would be going too far to suggest that a data scientist with a PhD in advanced maths would be predisposed to analytical thinking and that a business leader who has been working in a given domain for the last 15 years would favour a more intuitive way of thinking.

Connecting these two types of thinking and the ability to do so effectively will provide the competitive advantage for messy teams across businesses in the future.

I have looked at this new paradigm extensively through my military and business experiences, based upon the new environment that both worlds now face. Through speaking to numerous leaders involved in this change, I call for leadership development efforts to look different as per Figure 14 on the next page.

FIGURE 14: DEVELOPING LEADERS IN A NEW WAY...

FROM	TO
Classroom-based training programs driven by theory and models	Building thinking skills through case-study-based training and experiences
Head down and focus on executing the plan	Facilitate an environment of open inquiry and debate
'Sign and seal' the plan. No changes!	Defer reaching conclusions for as long as possible
Focus on my team's part in the plan and flawlessly execute	Consider different perspectives from other teams in the business
Let's all align and agree before we go anywhere!	Let's iterate as we go
Authority sits with the boss	Leaders are receptive to objections and challenges
Seek harmony and consensus	Encourage alternative views – embrace a devil's advocate
Keep a close-knit team of 'friends'	Integrate expert skill sets and external viewpoints
Knowledge is power	Maintain an enthusiasm for sharing

BUILDING TRUST BETWEEN DOMAIN AND ANALYTICS SKILLS

#1 ALIGN TO WHAT'S IMPORTANT

Using your purpose as a handrail for discovery, build a shared understanding of the team's ambitions. Allocate time to interpret, challenge and understand this context. Be open to debate around this, but the primacy is on the team here, not on the individual.

When researching for this book, I interviewed a US Navy Seal and we discussed the gap between the data people and the business people in the teams that he has served. He said that the gap is the least visible the stronger the focus and clarity on the mission. Here, domain and analytics titles are irrelevant, as everyone shares the same heightened level of focus.

The *Harvard Business Review 2012* article, "Data Scientist: The Sexiest Job of the 21st Century" got the data science profession off to a bad start. Yes, they are a new skill set. Yes, we need them. But we must help integrate them into business teams or they will be placed on separate projects away from what matters.

INTRODUCTION

PART ONE

CHAPTER 1

CHAPTER 2

CHAPTER 3

CHAPTER 4

PART TWO

CHAPTER 5

CHAPTER 6

CHAPTER 7

PART THREE

CHAPTER 8

CHAPTER 9

CHAPTER 10 / CONCLUSION

#2 REMOVE RANK AND POWER

The leader in the information age is a facilitator for discussions. Leaders should ensure that they are staging the right discussion and posing the right questions, allowing authority to shift back and forth between analytics and domain experience in the team. The perception of "I'm in charge here" or "It's my project" is not good. Clarifying responsibility and ownership is fine, but move on swiftly.

#3 COMMUNICATION

Face-to-face communication: walk down the corridor, stage the meeting in a room, coffee shop or park green. It doesn't matter, but do not let technology get in the way. Rely on the thinking muscles of the team, not electronic means. For remote teams, this is the same (if this isn't too much of an oxymoron). Use technology to stage the right discussion: a what-if analysis or war gaming will trigger the right thinking in teams wherever they are in the world – through technology. Challenge and debate must still remain.

#4 CHALLENGE GROUPTHINK

We have all been subject to peer pressure from a young age in different forms, and while this pressure to conform can be a positive one, too much conformity will inhibit a team's ability to challenge its collective understanding and integrate data and analytical thinking into its decision-making process.

Organizations want employees to be 'one team' and align around a common set of behaviours. As I have described in previous chapters, this is a good thing.

United behaviours = :)

United thinking = :(

However, leaders need to be aware of the dangers of groupthink that can shortcut this, so that the team's decision is not challenged. Overcoming groupthink requires acceptance of authentic dissent – which can be so difficult, as groups often shun dissenters. As data scientists start to operate within teams and offer alternative perspectives, the dynamics and rituals of the team have to accommodate and be prepared for this challenge. If no one listens to and accommodates the alternative viewpoint, all will be lost and millions of dollars squandered as you skip to your next meeting.

As data scientists use a highly specialized language, it sometimes can be unintelligible to those unaware of its context and application. This is a particular challenge to a team that is working across cultural borders. These teams' communication skills depend ultimately on their ability to understand 'what is meant' rather than 'what is being said'.

THE LEADERSHIP CHALLENGE

The role of the leader in such complex and uncertain situations now turns to setting the right environment and conditions to stage the required broad range of thinking skills to get the best thinking from their people and their organizations. I believe that this type of leadership actually enables teams to think for themselves, to develop ideas and coordinate in a bottom-up manner. Here is the means of executing leadership through the social mechanisms and cultural orientation that encourages challenge and debate, develops trust and stimulates discovery-driven thinking and creativity.

KEY CONSIDERATIONS FOR TEAMS

How can we get messy?

- How can technology help us, but not impede building our thinking skills?
- How can we ask better questions as a team?
- How are we managing bias, groupthink and heuristics?
- What are our team rituals? Can we name them?

_____

_____

_____

_____

_____

_____

CHAPTER 9

SITUATIONAL AWARENESS IN TEAMS

Customer Obsession:
Leaders start with the customer
and work backwards.

Amazon Leadership Principals

In 2003, a blackout hit the entire Northeast region of the US. It did not result from lack of power, or any inability to generate electricity. At a time of rising demand for electricity – a hot August day – the various electric companies were not able to share information about routing power on the grid and, lacking situational awareness, made the wrong decisions, which led to the massive electricity shutdown.[50]

Failures like this happen in business when situational awareness is not maintained and when teams are not on the same page, but operating in silos and focusing on executing the plan that's in front of them.

Continuous commitment to building situational awareness is absolutely essential to the success of a data-driven team. This situational awareness provides greater comprehension (insight) of the problem; applying judgment to this comprehension provides understanding of the problem (foresight). Foresight will never be perfect, but improving the quality of a team's questions and interactions with data and the analysis of it will make it more certain.

In a business with a data-driven culture, there is situational awareness throughout, from the front lines to operations to management. Data provide the insights about the situation and, combined with other sources, provide the material from which experience and judgment produce decisions. Situational awareness is a fundamental part of understanding.

50 US-Canada Power System Outage Task Force, "Final Report on the August 14, 2003 Blackout," April 2004, last accessed on August 25, 2017 https://energy.gov/sites/prod/files/oeprod/Documentsand Media/Blackout Final-Web.pdf

WHAT IS SITUATIONAL AWARENESS?

The classic concept of situational awareness was defined by Texas Tech Professor Mica R. Endsley in 1995, and has since been accepted by most experts.[51] Endsley explained that situational awareness is more than just seeing and hearing what is going on around you.

"Situational awareness is the perception of the elements in the environment within a volume of time and space, the comprehension of their meaning and the projection of their status in the near future," according to Endsley. "It means understanding the integrated meaning of perceptions in light of goals."

51 Mica R. Endsley, "Situational Awareness," *Human Factors*, 37(1), 32-64

The purpose of situational awareness is to translate data into intelligence, ahead of events, trends and evolution. By monitoring everything that affects the business – consumer trends, market evolution, events, changes to the competition, rises and falls in the economy and so on – the team stays ahead of the customers, rather than stumbling behind them to keep up. Data alone is worth nothing; turning it into intelligence is where the real value can be found.

But it should be clear that situational awareness is part of understanding, not understanding itself. Situational awareness is the 'appreciation' of what is happening, but not necessarily 'why' it is happening. Experience, education, judgment and knowledge all contribute to understanding.

Teams must establish situational awareness and maintain it in a continuous effort through everyday interactions and meetings. We have been taught that a 'good meeting' is all about a well-crafted aim and agenda. These are table stakes when it comes to building the required level of situational awareness needed to see around corners. Team members share the responsibility, and each has a separate role to challenge each other, groupthink and bias. This means that team members must trust each other and be open to challenge and debate.

IT'S LIKE FLYING A PLANE

The example of how a flight crew operates is useful in understanding this concept. As pilots, co-pilots and other members of the flight crew prepare for takeoff, they seek to obtain in advance all relevant information about the flight, building a mental picture and updating that image by keeping everyone in the information loop.

This means taking into account all that is going on with the aircraft and its immediate flight environment. This means determining what will happen in the near future (foresight) based on elements in the environment and the comprehension of their meaning, to paraphrase Endsley.

To obtain this awareness, the crew must: Focus on the relevant information in the environment and extract it; integrate it with applicable knowledge; create a mental 'picture' of the situation; determine, from the 'picture', what future events may be expected that may affect the flight.

Flight crews call this 'keeping in the loop', and it means that every decision the pilot or crew takes must be evaluated for results and consequences, in the light of the evolving situation. When the desired outcome has not been obtained, the current information must be updated and adjustments made.

One pilot puts it in simple terms: "I have a specific assignment in terms of situational awareness that my team depends on. It includes asking:

- **Location**
  Where are you in space, not only laterally, i.e., 12 miles southeast of ABC VOR, but in four dimensions? You need to work in the present altitude (and rate of climb or descent), airspeed, heading/track and course intent, all as they relate to your flight plan, which might include crossing or other altitude or speed restrictions. All these factors are critical to understanding the nature of your present situation and what future actions you might need to take in the normal or adapted course of the flight.

- **Angle of Attack**
  What is your current energy state? Modern displays usually include a trend vector indicator that gives valuable information about where on the energy curve you currently reside. This is a critical part of situational awareness, especially as you get lower to the ground.

- **Traffic**

  Where is the other traffic? How will it affect the safety of flight not only now but as you progress along your route of flight?

- **Terrain**

  Where is the high terrain? How will it affect your future flight path? ForeFlight Mobile Pro features a cool profile view that shows you how your flight-planned route and altitudes relate to upcoming terrain. Lacking such technology, this is the kind of visual image you need to create in your own mind to manage your relationship to high terrain.

- **Fuel and Equipment**

  That destination 2.4 hours away is imaginary if you have but two hours of fuel on board. Fuel reserves (along with other consumables, such as oxygen or de-icing fluid) plus constant systems monitoring are critical parts of the overall calculation."

Often a crew can lose situational awareness if they are concentrating on other things, so it is crucial to analyse whether or not they took a reasonable course of action in foresight, not in hindsight. Also recall that if crews are distracted by other important events, the time and effort they have to spend on the situational awareness processes are low, the pilot notes. That explains the loss of situational awareness, but it does not explain why they prioritized the way that they did. Such analysis should be seriously attempted.

Conditions leading to the loss of situational awareness may include the following:

- **Ambiguity** – information from multiple sources that do not agree
- **Fixation** – focusing on one thing; attentional focus/tunnelling
- **Confusion** – uncertainty or bafflement about a situational
- Not **prioritizing** the requisite tasks – everyone is focused on other activities that relate to them
- Everyone's **'heads down'** in action, failing to observe what's around them
- Cannot resolve **discrepancies** – contradictory data or personal conflicts
- Not **communicating** fully and effectively – vague or incomplete statements

But research has shown that lost or reduced situational awareness is a term that sometimes gets used very generally, often without much analysis. It is easy to identify in hindsight that the crew did not know something important, but much more challenging to discover why, and determine if the circumstances could have been reasonably foreseen and generalized to other situations.

This happens in business meetings all the time.

THE SITUATIONALLY AWARE TEAM

The flow of information from the front lines to the centre, the clarity of direction from the centre, and the flow of insights from all around the company should produce teams that are situationally aware. In other words, teams whose members know what they need to know, given their responsibilities.

It's an ongoing process. Keen situational awareness is a multidimensional process that continuously acquires, evaluates and applies information as new input, new opportunities, new threats, new strengths and new vulnerabilities appear, impinge and attack.

For situational awareness to be built by the team, team members must first develop trust. Each team member must be confident that the others are doing their jobs, so that the information the entire team needs to share is complete and requisite. This also provides assurance that information and insights shared with the rest of the company will be based on good input.

This can be difficult when new members join the team from a very different field and the quickest way to establish this trust is to be clear on the goal. Unifying data and business leaders around this and building a shared responsibility for it immediately builds trust. It removes emotion and ownership, and clarifies a shared purpose.

Team members should also share values, so that their approach to any problem is based on the same principles. Interaction with the leadership helps instil corporate culture in each team member, so that each member knows exactly where the company is headed and what its objectives are. They should also be ready to fail and learn together. Sharing that experience with the rest of the company helps it to move forward together.

Authority should also be shared, and that includes the team leaders. There should be a continuing discussion underway about the situation, and the foresight that comes from understanding it. Should the team leader not be up to speed on some aspect of this, the team should be able to bring the leader up to speed without fear of challenge.

It is critical that discussions based on the questions "where are we now" and "where are we headed" continuously take place, so that the latest insights from data guide the team's actions.

The team should also continually exchange ideas and get access to the strategic centre. The headquarters of the British military has changed the way that its generals are briefed and updated. Previously, subject-matter experts at a lower rank would brief their boss, who would then pass it up the chain of command, with each leader adding their personal interpretation of the data to it, thus diluting the quality of insight from the front line. This has since changed, and senior military generals ask specifically to meet with subject-matter experts to share with them front-line situations and insights. In doing so, through such a simple ritual, the hierarchy of the headquarters was flattened in a second.

In every organization there are, of course, those individuals who play the political game and control these vertical information flows. Removing these individuals from the organization may be necessary, as they will stifle the understanding and situational awareness the organization requires.

Dell provides a good example of successful situational awareness. Dell was able to change the pricing on a product in a single day, neutralizing a potential customer insurgency, thanks to its ongoing awareness of customer trends.

The computer manufacturer uses social media tools to stay close to customers, but also to share insights from data with the entire company. Dell has a permanent Social Media Command Centre that monitors conversation and activity for every one of its products across all social channels. What sets Dell apart are the relationships between the Command Centre and the lines of business. The communications channels enable the teams to respond quickly to what is observed in the marketplace.[52]

52 "Dell has a Social Media Command Center," last modified December 8, 2010 https://blog.dell. com/en-us/dell-s- next-step-the-social- media-listening- command-center/

"The old adage 'The sum is greater than the parts' is nowhere more applicable than in the business world today. Yet breaking down organizational barriers and sharing information seems to be a recurring problem for most organizations," writes management expert Scott Leeb. "Lessons learned often become simply lessons *heard* because they are presented when individuals cannot leverage the insights to drive smarter decision-making. The key is to share information readily so it is available on-demand and develop processes and procedures so that sharing becomes part of the DNA of an organization. In turn, accessing the insights when they are needed, as opposed to when they are presented, becomes a driver for improved decision-making."[53]

53 "Decision-Making Top-Gun Style," Harvard Business Review, September 2013 last accessed August 25, 2017 https://hbr.org/2013/09/decision-making-top-gun-style

KEY CONSIDERATIONS FOR TEAMS

How can we maintain situational awareness?

- How can we continuously look ahead using data?
- How can we avoid getting stuck in the here and now?
- Are we just looking at data or turning it into meaningful intelligence?
- How do we keep our team members 'in the loop'?

CHAPTER 10

ASKING BETTER QUESTIONS

Innovation is not about coming up with good ideas, but coming up with good questions.

You have your data. You have the technology to analyse it. Now, do you know what to ask?

You want to know more about your customers, and what's driving them. But even a simple question about 'customers' needs to be qualified. Their actions? Their spending? Their expectations?

At Caesars Entertainment Corp., the Las Vegas-based international gaming company, it became clear that language choices mattered in agreeing on data interpretation. The company was trying to develop a scorecard for its hotels, as part of its initiative to improve energy efficiency and make them environmentally friendly. Among managers, contention quickly arose over the specific information to include in the scorecard.

Some stakeholders thought the scorecard should highlight progress toward cost-reduction and financial goals, which led to debates over whether to track energy consumption or cost savings. Other stakeholders then asked if it was fair to compare older buildings with newer ones built to greener specifications. What about buildings located in hot climates? Was it fair to compare them with buildings in more moderate zones without adjusting for temperature differences?[54]

This is why clarity of language is a key factor in a data-driven corporate culture. If your query to the data is too general, then the insights gleaned may not be applicable.

Defining terms like 'customer' carefully will, on the other hand, lead to useful insights. Is it someone who has been

54 "Lessons from becoming a data driven organization," last modified October 18, 2016 http://sloanreview. mit.edu/case-study/ lessons-from- becoming-a-data- driven-organization/

active in the last six months? Or someone who spent a certain amount of money? Making this clear will make a huge difference for data experts as they share back the results with their business leaders. If the semantics are wrong, credibility will be instantly lost – no matter how solid the model.

CASE STUDY – R.R. DONNELLY

DISRUPTING LOGISTICS

Defining the Challenge

R.R. Donnelly is a Fortune 500 marketing and communications group – the company manages every form of communication, from email to freight hauling to logistics.

As R.R. Donnelley grew its shipping business, it increasingly found itself in an excellent position to capture a wide range of market segments. But providing accurate rates was critical to the growth of the business. As the business grew, R.R. Donnelley found that providing accurate rates to the satisfaction of its customers had become more complex.

Asking the Right Questions

R. R. Donnelly wasn't asking the right questions. Either they would estimate too high or too low, because they weren't able to use the data to their advantage. The company admits that they just didn't understand all the variables. But they knew they were losing business.

With the problem identified, the business group turned to outside expertise in analytics to resolve the problem. The decision was made to build a 'rate engine', an algorithm that would predict rates with razor-fine accuracy.

A team was put together, a collaborative effort among the company's data scientists and experts from the front lines, from a number of the company's business verticals. By bringing in analytics experts from outside the transportation industry, R.R. Donnelly got a new perspective on rates, which it could use in conjunction with its own expertise from all around the company.

The rate engine is a big-data analytics system that leverages machine learning to process data. The system is built on a machine-learning platform to use historical data for a complex multivariate, forward-looking model. In other words, the data includes everything the company has about shipping and pricing, going back as far as possible. Then variables are added like weather, market trends, physical capability of transportation – anything that could possibly relate to shipping.

This has led to cultural change. R.R. Donnelly has undergone what it calls a shift in thinking that has changed the culture of the company as it increasingly shares information across silos to get the best from the data. The tool's development also provided a largely unexpected opportunity for cross-team collaboration, according to company sources.

The Results Show Accuracy
The result was that the truckload win rate increased by 4% and paid for itself in the first month of deployment, according to an announcement by the company.

In 2017, according to the company's financial results announcement, they project that their truckload brokerage business will grow from $4 million to $16 million. That is a $12 million or 2% increase in revenue, which is worth $600 million in total revenue for the business.

The first-of-its-type rate engine, which placed second in the 2017 *InformationWeek* Excellence Awards in Data and Analytics, predicts truckload rates in real time and is 7.5-times more accurate than the industry average, company sources say. The rate engine is continually updated with new data from both statistics and from front-line observations, so that it becomes ever-more reliable and accurate. At the *InformationWeek* Excellence Awards, the company said that the new rate engine has disrupted and redefined the industry's standards for rate modelling.

There have been a number of ancillary benefits that the engine and the cultural change have produced. Speed is one advantage, as the company can now respond to quotes very rapidly, without any kind of manual verification. Time-consuming manual checking of figures was making the company late for potential business. Another bidder could intervene in the interim.

Another benefit, one the company didn't anticipate, is the cultural change. Now the company is discovering the possibilities of using analytics and machine learning in other parts of the business. The company took the time and trouble to get everyone on board for these new concepts. Now it can profit from the ability to share information across the different operations.

So how do you get the leader who thinks about the 'up and out', the broader picture, and uses different types of language hundreds of times a day in hundreds of conversations with different types of people, to asking a focused and better question to data?

The first step is to align to what's important. Business and data leaders and teams need to be aligned towards what is going to drive the data collection effort. **The centre of this is understanding.**

For the military, an intelligence requirement is aimed at increasing understanding. Instead of going straight to the data, first formulate the right question.

For example, in Afghanistan, an intelligence officer and commander would formulate intelligence requirements – a question that when answered would provide us with a coherent level of understanding on a particular subject/theme. This then informs operational decisions. The key here is that intelligence is synthesized information/data that has gone through the process of integration and analysis.

For example: "How does the XX receive support from the local population in XX?"

We would then break this down into chunks of information or a single question, which when processed and integrated with other information forms a level of understanding on a subject (intelligence) in order to inform operational planning. On its own, an information requirement can provide a fact, but not understanding, about a subject. Information requirements are the building blocks of intelligence requirements.

Continuing the example above: "Where are the XX safe houses? How does the local population provide financial support to XX?"

From here, what data to collect is easy. Information (data points), when linked together, should provide an answer to an information requirement. These data points are usually built from indicators of an information requirement. An example of this is if we wanted to know where the safe houses of XX fighters in XX were, we might make a list of what kinds of locations might be used as safe houses and these would form indicators for the presence of safe houses. The locations by themselves are useless unless we have the context of how they are being used – both of these bits of data together would help make an assessment of where the safe houses were (e.g., overnight locations, family member locations, friend locations, mosques associated with XX, meeting locations).

Industrializing this language proved to be critical to allow analysts and data scientists to operate at a faster pace and, as the tour went on, understanding grew.

Remember that today, businesses win if they have the ability to understand better than their competitors.

It is then up to the data scientist to look at the data, and to identify trends, market evolution and customer segmentation – to provide an overall picture of the company's situation and status. Here the CDO must work with the front lines to identify issues (intelligence requirements) and formulate them for analysis.

CASE STUDY
– APIXIO

DISRUPTING ASKING THE RIGHT QUESTIONS OF DATA IN HEALTHCARE

Founded in 2009, Apixio is the data science company for healthcare. Apixio's platform extracts and analyzes clinical data in electronic health records, generating insights into patient health, with the objective of delivering better care.

The challenge in healthcare is to ask the right questions of the data. Physicians depend on electronic health records (EHRs), and studies show that critical information is often missing from these records or diagnostic codes are missing or incorrect.[55]

Moreover, much diagnostic experience comes from long-term medical studies or clinical trials. Much medical

55 "Clinical Decision Support Systems for Improving Diagnostic Accuracy," Journal of Clinical Bioinformatics, 5: 4

knowledge has resulted from the time and money spent on such studies, but knowledge can also be patchy in areas where studies are lacking. Clinical trials work by testing new treatments in small groups at first, looking at how well the treatment works and identifying any side effects. In order to safeguard participants and improve reliability, clinical trials have to meet rigorous scientific standards. However, that's not to say there is no risk of methodological flaws, or that the smallish populations used in clinical trials always generalize well outside of a particular study.

This is where big data can help. By mining the world of practice-based clinical data – i.e., actual patient records – for information on who has what condition and what treatments are working, we could learn a lot about the way we care for individuals.

By gathering information that exists on specific geographic areas, and making use of information that is not easily tapped, big data can provide a whole new perspective on medical and pharmaceutical issues. Dr Eric Schadt, the founding director of the Icahn Institute for Genomics and Multiscale Biology at New York's Mount Sinai Health System, told McKinsey: "The role of big data in medicine is one where we can build better health profiles and better predictive models around individual patients so that we can better diagnose and treat disease."[56]

In other words, framing the right questions and going to the data to get answers. "By mining the world of practice-based clinical data – who has what condition and what treatments are working – organizations can learn a lot about the way they care for individuals," comments Apixio CEO Darren Schulte.[57]

56 "The Role of Big Data in Medicine," last modified; No date available. http://www.mckinsey.com/industries/pharmaceuticals-and-medical-products/our-insights/the-role-of-big-data-in-medicine

57 "PMlive News," last modified February 2, 2017 http://www.pmlive.com/pharma_intelligence/mining_for_results_1184909

FRAMING THE QUESTIONS

About 80% of medical data is unstructured – notes by physicians, email, hospital records, Medicare records, etc. Data is scattered and not necessarily included in electronic health records (EHRs). They include only a subset of relevant data, and crucial information is often buried in text-based case notes, scanned documents and other unstructured data sources.

The EHRs themselves are often riddled with errors, particularly in terms of diagnostic codes (a shorthand for illnesses and conditions) and they are the basis of decision-making for medical personnel. They are a key element of risk management, and they affect care delivery optimization, outcomes measurement, reimbursement and more.

Yet, despite the importance of accurate diagnostic coding, studies show that more than 60% of key clinical information is missing from the coded layer of the EHR, and 30% to 50% of the information in the EHRs structured problem list is spurious.[58] Healthcare organizations do make checks and reviews of EHRs to find errors, but only a small percentage are ever corrected.

Apixio can process all this data, from EHRs and other sources, and can validate it using other sources. Using its dedicated platforms, Apixio can create a model for a single patient, or for a patient segment, or an even broader division of the population, finding disease prevalence and treatment patterns.

Apixio creates models using data obtained by text processing and mining texts, deriving patterns from the data in much the same way that the military does when it seeks activity patterns. In this way, Apixio can answer questions about what works and what doesn't in personalized medicine and in public health issues.

"This can have an effect on individual care, reducing the number of doctor visits a patient requires, the number of times a patient becomes sick, the number of times a patient has progressed into a given disease state. All should diminish," comments Schadt.

58 "The Role of Big Data in Medicine," last modified; No date available. http://www.mckinsey.com/industries/pharmaceuticals-and-medical-products/our-insights/the-role-of-big-data-in-medicine

GETTING THE ANSWERS

INTRODUCTION
PART ONE
CHAPTER 1
CHAPTER 2
CHAPTER 3
CHAPTER 4
PART TWO
CHAPTER 5
CHAPTER 6
CHAPTER 7
PART THREE
CHAPTER 8
CHAPTER 9
CHAPTER 10 / CONCLUSION

San Diego-based Scripps Health Plan Services (SHPS) is one organization that's getting the answers it needs from Apixio's healthcare analytics. SHPS runs a top-ranked integrated health system with four hospitals, a network of outpatient centers and clinics, and more than 2,600 affiliated physicians. SHPS enrols approximately 93,000 members through plan-to-plan agreements with other health plans.

Using Apixio's technology to comb through electronic health records, SHPS has found a fast, flexible and cost-effective way to find uncoded and wrongly coded conditions. Examining the charts of more than 21,000 Medicare Senior Advantage members, Apixio identified and confirmed 750 additional conditions. Those previously unidentified codes offer potential improvements to patient care, system efficiency, revenue and institutional risk. Now, performance improvement leaders at SHPS are identifying new areas where they can apply the Apixio solution.[59]

Another company that has learned to frame questions differently, thanks to Apixio, is the San Ramon, California-based Hill Physicians Medical Group. The group transitioned from manually pulling charts and finding information on them to direct EHR extraction.

Direct extraction improves physician engagement, because it saves time and ensures information accuracy. Apixio finds all the relevant unstructured data for the physicians, and then processes it so that they secure the necessary information.

Apixio's ability to frame the questions for the physicians, validate the data and provide the requisite insights has improved efficiency and accuracy in the group's healthcare organization.

---

59 Chris Gough, "Solving Practical Problems with Healthcare Analytics," Apixio White Paper February 2016 https://www.apixio.com/wp-content/uploads/2016/02/Intel-Health-Apixio-white-paper-LR-1.pdf

Most of the time, management falls in between the extremes of knowing specific issues to investigate and not knowing anything at all. With basic orientation, predictive analytics can isolate the relevant customer trends from the masses of data and provide foresight on what will happen next. As trends are identified, analysis can drill down to more specific levels – i.e., customers are buying certain gifts, towards customer X will buy a camera.

So, it's not about starting with a gut instinct and looking for a data report to prove or disprove it – that's Little League stuff. Data-driven teams will start with "What do we need to understand?" This is a skill gap that currently exists and the starting point is to help teams interact effectively with data through a simple and common language.

Leaders need to get these questions right. Consider the well-known story of two CEOs at the same company. The first CEO tried to use big-data analytics to define strategy. But he asked the wrong questions, and earnings fell 25% in one year. That CEO was replaced by the second one, who was more skilled at using the data. He turned the company around in one year.

How is it possible that two experienced executives can view the same data so differently? Understanding how to get the data to help you frame questions for further investigation is critical.

For example, at Anthem, a leading US provider of healthcare benefits and insurance, it was necessary to reconcile definitions of emergency-room visits that varied across the 14 regions it serves, before it could begin going to the data.

And the Bank of England, ahead of announcing housing policy recommendations, was obliged to harmonize terminology across departments before analysing the data required to make the policy decisions.[60]

60 Michael Fitzgerald, "Better Data brings a Renewal at the Bank of England," Sloan Review, May 26, 2016, last accessed on August 25, 2016 http://sloanreview. mit.edu/case-study/ better-data-brings-a- renewal-at-the-bank- of-england/

THE ANALYSIS PROCESS

With the questions established, there is the process of defining the data and writing the code for extracting and manipulating the data. Data may also be in unstructured and special formats, so that it has to be manipulated, matched and cross-referenced. It has to reach the required quality standards to be analysed.

The ability to succeed depends in part on the data maturity within the organization: how long have they been collecting data, how sophisticated is the collection and management process, and how is the data cleaned and stored?

Those with a long history of data management and sophistication in handling data are likely to have very specific and clear questions for how they want to use it. They will have a lot of systems in place, along with experience in handling them. On the other hand, a company that has only just started to collect data recently, or one that may not have had any data of their own, will have to plan for more data collection before they can even get started. And they may not be very sophisticated at all in asking the right questions.

When a company is in this situation, then going to the data is like "looking in a global ocean for an object that might or might not be a fish. It might be anything and it might be important, but at first, we are not sure if it even exists. And whatever it might be, it will be constantly moving and interacting with a huge number of other objects. They might make up an organized school of fish or they might not be related at all. But we do know that we need to find it, identify what it is and figure out how it relates to all the other objects – we either know or think might be important," as one military expert puts it.[61]

Starting from scratch, or nearly that, asking the data questions simply leads to more questions. With sophisticated analytical tools, the first questions will lead to more detailed and specific ones, as per the example above.

One limitation that may need to be overcome is expanding the usual vocabulary that is the internal language of the business' employees. Most businesses develop a kind of technical language of their own, half jargon, half expressions that come from the market or the industry. Sometimes it is difficult for leaders to think outside this limited range of concepts, but they will need to do this if they are to frame the questions that get the best answers from the data.

61 Chandler P. Atwood, "Activity-Based Intelligence: Revolutionizing Military Intelligence Analysis," Joint Force Quarterly 77, 2nd Quarter April 2015, last accessed August 25, 2017 http://ndupress. ndu.edu/JFQ/Joint-Force-Quarterly-77/ Article/581866/ activity-based-intelligence-revolutionizing-military-intelligence-analysis/

Often, the intervention of a business analyst can be an obstacle to expanding the range of concepts as much as needed. The business analyst may be tasked with gathering information for the analyst. This is never advisable, as the business analyst may not have the in-depth knowledge of the business that the data scientist requires. Yet the business analyst does the talking with different parts of the organization and defines what needs to be done. The lack of detail and nuances can skew the analysis definitively.

One way to avoid this kind of issue is for the leader to engage in ongoing dialogue with the data scientist. This allows the scientist to get to know the details of the business, the leader's concerns and upcoming issues, and seek understanding. For example, the scientist may observe that he's noticed that a client hasn't spent anything in X number of months, or a particular client has had very low-level transactions. This may suggest other ideas to the leader that may be worth exploring based on his intelligence requirement. It should be a back-and-forth process and break business unit and geographic boundaries – *I know that a team in another part of the business has a similar intelligence require-ment; these insights might help them.* It should be an iterative process as well, so that work goes on until the key insights are found.

Both the leader and the analyst must constantly seek to discover by managing any pre-set mindsets or bias. A prejudiced approach can skew the analysis from the start, and then nothing worthwhile will emerge. Under-standing and clarity are critical from both sides. If the analysts get a wrong start because of bias in that area or action, they can waste a huge amount of time ana-lysing the data without it being useful in any way. By achieving this accuracy at the start, it will make their time so much more efficient and they will be able to ask much more specific questions of the business leader. Otherwise, they just get lost in the huge amounts of data that they're dealing with.

Accuracy around language is equally important when you're talking about results or presenting results to teams. It should be clear to leaders and the team that the frameworks discussed at the start were used in the right context throughout the analysis.

KEY CONSIDERATIONS FOR TEAMS

How can we ask better questions?

- Are we clear and aligned to what we want to understand?
- What focused questions do we need to ask to build or maintain this understanding?
- How can this be broken down into data points?
- Who else in the organization (another team?) has found success with this data?
- How can we learn from them?
- How can we exploit this advantage?

CONCLUSION

COMPANIES DON'T KNOW WHAT THEY KNOW

The greatest opportunity for organizations to have a competitive advantage in the big-data world is simple and available to any team that wants it.

As I have shared with you in this book, when organizations move into a period of heightened uncertainty and complexity, with the buzz of market activity, customers and competitors surrounding them, and a host of different threats and opportunities, it will be those that establish the right data culture that will succeed in achieving their goals.

Teams need to simply align to what's important for them and focus on their purpose and how they are going to use data to add value for the people they serve. This is the handrail for data discovery and when you get lost in all the noise of analytics and insights and complicated tools – go back to this.

Teams need to master interactions with big data by formulating better questions. A forward-looking, discovery-driven mindset will fuel innovation and adaptability as teams move away from command and control and centralized planning processes that impeded this great opportunity. And finally, teams need to translate their insights to other teams in their network.

The synchronicity of experience and data is where true advantage lies. Business experience and gut instinct alone are not enough. Locking data scientists away on projects will simply isolate this exciting new talent. Bring them into everyday challenges and debates with business leaders, where conversations are hypothesis-led, and assumptions and bias are challenged, and they can see the business value of their work. The team comes first here, not the executive.

I frequently think of the men and women whose lives changed that day on my military convoy, due to injury or who made the ultimate sacrifice. It is to them that I would like to pay my respects. If I had asked more questions, then, there might have been a different outcome. If the organization had been better at translating insights up and down the command chain to the front line, there might have been a different outcome.

On these pages, I wanted to share with you my story. And I hope, that wherever you are, you're inspired to think in a different way.

Start now. At your next meeting …

AN INTRODUCTION TO GRAHAM HOGG

GRAHAM has spent the last 15 years inspiring leaders and teams to anchor data into everyday decision making. He began his career as a Royal Marines Officer, specializing in Intelligence. This experience led Graham to the belief that building understanding in teams through the lens of an organization's purpose will lead to better decisions. He believes that the right synchronization of experience and data is crucial to achieve this.

Graham has devoted his life to sharing his thinking in order to help teams inside organizations ask better questions to data. As the leader of Connectworxs, he is passionate about helping organizations achieve growth by creating the right data driven behaviours to achieve their ambitions.

Graham lives in New York with his young family.

100% of the Author's royalties will be donated to military charities in the UK and US.